CREATIVITY
AT WORK

CREATIVITY AT WORK

Supercharge your brain and make your ideas stick

Ros Taylor

KoganPage

LONDON PHILADELPHIA NEW DELHI

First published in Great Britain and the United States in 2013 by Kogan Page Limited
Reprinted 2013 (twice)

2nd Floor, 45 Gee Street
London EC1V 3RS
United Kingdom
www.koganpage.com

1518 Walnut Street, Suite 1100
Philadelphia PA 19102
USA

4737/23 Ansari Road
Daryaganj
New Delhi 110002
India

© Ros Taylor 2013

ISBN   978 0 7494 6666 4
E-ISBN   978 0 7494 6667 1

British Library Cataloguing-in-Publication Data

A CIP record for this book is available from the British Library.

Library of Congress Cataloging-in-Publication Data

Taylor, Ros.
  Creativity at work : supercharge your brain and make your ideas stick / Ros Taylor.
    pages cm
    ISBN 978-0-7494-6666-4 – ISBN 978-0-7494-6667-1 (ebk.)   1. Creative ability in business.   2. Creative thinking.   I. Title.
    HD53.T39 2013
    650.1–dc23
                                                                          2013006075

Typeset by Graphicraft Limited, Hong Kong
Printed and bound in Great Britain by CPI Group (UK) Ltd, Croydon, CR0 4YY

This book is dedicated to my husband John Young who has supported me throughout the writing of this book, especially during our holiday in France. I must also thank my friends whose responses are in the book or who suggested wonderful work creatives for me to interview.

Contents

PART II   The brain   59

PART III   Results   93

PART IV   Supercharging your workplace   123

Discover adjacent possibles   125

Creative environments   131

Creative skills for the workplace   149

PART V   The creative process   171

Using a creative process   173

The CREATE process   180

The final fling   194

Introduction

I certainly never thought of myself as creative. I sang and performed in opera but I didn't paint or compose or direct. That to me was 'true' creativity. I certainly didn't see my work as a psychologist as remotely creative despite having to plan therapeutic programmes for each patient I saw.

Creativity was someone else, somewhere else. My partner at the time was gloriously creative, writing books on entrepreneurship and producing musicals. By comparison I felt unworthy. He discovered the Creative Problem Solving Institute in Buffalo, home to Osborn and Parnes, the creators of brainstorming and the creative method. He would return from conferences with wonderfully wacky ideas. He told the story of a very large man with a very small triangle that he would strike intermittently and when you heard the 'ting' you had to blurt out the first thing that came into your head. The aim of this was to jolt people out of their entrenched thoughts. It all sounded impossibly romantic and 'out there' and not for the likes of me!

That relationship came to an end and I left Scotland to work in London. That summer I decided to go to Buffalo and experience the 'tings' for myself. I never did meet the large man with the small triangle but I did encounter some marvellous people and experiences. I have Sufi danced, painted large murals, danced with Brazilians, sung eight-part harmony with people who have never sung before and listened to the most creative speakers the world has to offer. In addition to these artistic experiences I also learnt about problem solving and how individuals and teams can come up with ideas whenever they require them. I began to understand how I was creative and what my unique offering is to the world of work. I also came to realize just how important ideas were to the lifeblood of a company and organization.

If there were ever a time that we require to do things differently it is now. I know in my own business, which focuses on leadership development and executive coaching, that many companies at times of financial challenge have less money to spend or just stop buying. So it has been up to all of us in our company to come up with different ways of delivering and unique ways of differentiating us in the marketplace.

Dr Richard Florida is one of the world's leading experts on economic competitiveness, demographic trends and cultural and technological innovation. He claims that developing the full human and creative capabilities of each individual, combined with institutional supports such as commercial innovation and new industry, will put us back on the path to economic and social prosperity. Like Richard, I think most people would agree that creativity at work is 'a good thing'. What with the recession, more people out of work and fewer jobs to go round, doing things differently would be right at the top of an organization's agenda you might think. But is it?

There are a number of paradoxes around at the moment. Politicians talk about the UK being a knowledge economy based on innovation, but it doesn't seem to have had an impact so far on our recovery. And why has the government cut back its research centres by 60 per cent if the priority right now is on innovation? Talking to clients, the word is that a focus on short-term shareholder value has created less time for creativity and doing things differently, not more. In addition the dodgy capitalism of the sort we have seen recently in banks may have reduced the appetite for the risk of new ways or new products.

However, I knew none of these things for certain. So I decided to find out with a mixture of 100 one-to-one interviews, online questionnaires and a more formal poll of 1,000 working people in the UK. I wanted to learn what they thought about creativity at work, what it looked like on the ground. I wanted to cut through the rhetoric and get down to what happens every day in companies and organizations that are faced with a changing customer base and volatile markets. Do employees feel empowered to come up with new ideas and are they rewarded for their input? Are HR departments hiring creative board members to move this creativity agenda forward? Did teams have a creative process so that they could produce ideas or solve problems swiftly and effectively?

I also discovered that there have been a number of myths about creativity that I think I had succumbed to myself:

- Creative people are eccentric personalities who are different from the rest of us.

- Creativity is really about the arts and has no place in everyday life and certainly not in either business or the professions.

- Creativity is a mysterious process that can't be studied as ideas come out of the blue with no traceable path.

- The greatest creativity comes from people working on their own, witness Archimedes and Sir Isaac Newton.

- It might be OK for the Googles of this world that have money to throw at creativity but not me in my small business.

These myths have been challenged by a robust body of research spearheaded by Teresa Amabile, Professor at Harvard Business School. But has this information percolated down to where it matters at the coal face of business? And what does creativity mean to a cross-section of business people and is their definition of creativity different from that of an artist? What do people do in organizations every day to harness ideas for business improvement? Can we learn anything from artists, designers or photographers who have to be creative for a living?

In this book I share my journey with you to find answers to these questions in the hope that you will take up the challenge of becoming even more creative than you are at the moment. It has taken longer than I thought as I kept discovering fascinating insights from neurology, psychology and business. The starting point really is that you can't be innovative at work without having creative ideas. When I started this enquiry I thought they were one and the same, a tautology. But I now know that they are not. Creativity is the precursor to innovation, the practical result – creativity made manifest.

So to begin I wanted to know if other leaders, consultants and artists were clear in their definition of what creativity is. I really like to see the whites of the eyes when I am researching a topic so out of the many respondents to an online questionnaire I circulated to our database, I chose 100 people from different sectors and countries and carried out telephone and face-to-face interviews. The open-ended questionnaire I used for these interviews follows in Chapter 1; do complete it yourself before I go on to reveal what my sample of 100 business people, artists and colleagues delivered. Some were sole traders or were working as consultants and directors of operas, etc so I asked them to think of a client organization where they were currently working or a team where they collaborated. I also asked them to complete a questionnaire I adapted called 'Your creative style' to see the range of difference in this sample. This is available in Chapter 4 of this book for you to complete so that you understand your contribution to creativity.

I then delved into the literature to see what happens in the brain. I wanted to know if creative thinking is different from other kinds of thinking and, if so, can this be measured and understood? I spent so long reading and delving that I had to be prised away to write this book. I began to wonder if my 100 people were a representative sample of attitudes to creativity at work so I put together a survey comprising 14 questions that look at three major areas of creativity at work: the resources organizations put into creative effort, the processes used to obtain new ideas, and finally the culture of an organization and how it can foster or drown creativity. This questionnaire is also included for you to complete; see Chapter 9.

'When in doubt find out' is my motto and the book is peppered with insights and exercises to build on your own creative style. Part I addresses how people define creativity and creativity at work and whether my sample of 100 felt themselves to be creative. I was also interested in who they thought were creative either as colleagues, family members or role models. I was also keen to register sector differences. Did bankers go about innovation in a different way from those in construction or the media? And did they see themselves as creative? Throughout I was looking for stories that would inspire all of us to do things differently.

Part II peels back the layers of the brain and peers into where thinking and ideas have their origin. I will examine how we make decisions and how perhaps we *should* make decisions. I am fascinated by the neurology of having an idea and what happens in the brain when we do. We are all such a mixture of paradoxes – built for conformity but with a glorious capacity for vision and change. When should we be alone to come up with ideas and when are we better in a group? Since I started this project so many people have told me that Einstein didn't have a team to work with, that Archimedes was alone in the bath and Picasso only had a model for company when painting. But they all had mates and it is certainly worth discussing how they got – and we get – ideas.

Part III delivers the results from the poll of 1,000 people at work I commissioned from Poll One. It asks 14 questions about their experience of creativity in their workplace; the results are broken down into job sector, male and female responses, senior and junior managers. The results are interesting and not good news for those of us who believe that market recovery is dependent on creativity and innovation happening constantly in organizations.

Part IV looks at what is necessary to foster a culture of creativity. That could be as a country, a company or a family. You are

10 times more likely to get an idea if you live in a city than in the country, we are told. So we look at the theory of 'the adjacent possible' in creativity as well as team creativity and creative leadership. Ideas need the petri dish of corporate agar to survive, so how can organizational environments get that right? You will hear about Teresa Amabile's recent research into company cultures that foster creativity and how that links to a government interest in our happiness.

Part V focuses on how we can be creative on demand. The access to or ability to use a process to foster creativity was in scarce supply. And while serendipity has an interesting part to play in creativity I am not sure organizations can wait for the bluebird of chance to alight on a project or product that has deadlines and tight windows of delivery. So a creative process will be suggested for use every day or certainly at weekly meetings. Our results show that most companies wait for the quarterly or annual meeting to 'be creative'; the away day where coming up with new ideas is sandwiched between paintballing or ice sculpting and getting drunk at the bar.

The objective of the book is to ensure that at the end you feel that you the reader are indeed creative. Dyer, Gregerson and Christensen, authors of *The Innovator's DNA* (Harvard Business School Press, 2011), reveal that if we *think* we are creative then we are more likely to *be* creative. So it is about changing a mind-set, *our* mind-set, realizing that everyone is creative, just in their own way. So that's the journey and the purpose. Enjoy the ride.

Definitions of creativity

I wanted to start the book by defining terms. What do we mean by creativity at work: how is it defined, who are creative work heroes and how creative do the people I interview think they are? The following chapters will confront these questions; perhaps you can form your own opinions and complete the same creativity at work questionnaire I gave to my group of 100; see below.

Creativity and undertakers

Mary Tomes is an undertaker. She inherited a business that could not have been more traditional but she was determined to do things differently. As she said when winning an Everywoman award, 'the funeral business had not changed for decades and really was long overdue for a new look'. So, with the help of her family, she launched Colourful Coffins. With Mary you can have any design on a coffin you want; you can even draw your own for a completely bespoke service – presumably before you die. These details were delivered over a lunch. Contrary to what you may think of as being ghoulish and off-putting, the audience were so captivated that a queue developed at the end of her speech with people booking their coffins in advance with their favourite colour. The woman next to me was securing bright pink to match her blouse!

▶

◀

> Sadly my mother died this year and I did ask the undertaker if she had colourful coffins in her repertoire. This suggestion was met with such profound horror that I gave up on the idea. But I know my mother would have loved a coffin in animal print. She was particularly fond of leopard skin. I mentioned this in her funeral oration and on the way out at the end a few of her friends sidled up to me to ask for details.
>
> So, taking something traditional and twisting the concept to provide a different service that appeals to customers – dead or alive – is at the heart of creativity.

When writing this book I was particularly keen to know what organizations were doing right now to be creative. Are there more Marys about with ideas in abundance? With so much literature about creativity and the creative process, I wanted to learn about the process of choice that is used in business today and the skills top teams and workforces employed to have new ideas and keep ahead of the competition. I also wanted to acquire qualitative information from a small cross-section of this group. These interviews were conducted face-to-face and by telephone. The questions are below. Do complete the questionnaire yourself.

Definitions of creativity

Let's look at my group's definitions. I have distilled the replies where there were commonalities of thought rather than provide you with all of them. I will share input from some of the experts I interviewed. Throughout Part I, I have highlighted interviews with selected leaders who made a difference to my thinking about creativity and the creative process at work.

Creativity at work questionnaire

What is your definition of creativity?

_____

_____

_____

Describe the most creative person you know.

_____

_____

_____

How creative do you think you are?

_____

_____

_____

What creative process would you use for coming up with new ideas or problem solving?

_____

_____

_____

When would you use that process? Once a week? Once a month? Once a year?

_____

_____

_____

Give some examples of creativity in your workplace.

_____

_____

_____

Creativity as artistic endeavour

There was specific focus on the arts in the majority of the group's definitions of creativity.

Ashley Pover, CEO of Met Zurich, brokers, maintains that any definition of creativity was 'not correlated to his marketplace'. He felt that it might exist elsewhere in business perhaps and certainly in the arts but not in *his* business. He goes out looking for new angles for client delivery but doesn't expect anyone else in the firm to do that. That sounded pretty creative to me.

Anne Fergusson, Senior Director at PWC, defines creativity as 'having the imagination to take something prosaic and make it beautiful. It's taking mankind a step further towards physical beauty to feed our souls'.

David Early, Manager with Babcock Marine, says creativity is 'The ability to express feelings by producing a tangible item, eg painting, sculpture, building.'

Debbie Lasrado of Mulgrave Heating suggests that, 'Creativity is about putting things across in a way which is different. It can be artistic, musically creative, or dramatically different. Not just sticking to the norm.'

Creativity is a virtual spaceman

Most responses were perhaps predictably about the generically new and different.

Bonnie Clarke, Director of Badenoch and Clark, said that the definition for her was 'Bringing everyday things and ideas to life in a different way.'

Susan Avarde, Director of Global Branding for Citigroup, felt it was about 'Bringing something new to the table and having a fresh view across the professions.'

David Hogarth, Finance Director of Deutsch Bank: 'a different view, a different angle to solutions'. Lisa Heneghan, Partner at KPMG said it was 'seeing with a different lens'. Leanne Smy of NPS Property Consultants defined it as 'out there'.

Francisco Negrin, Opera Director, summed up his view with: 'What you're doing is producing something new not just re-arranging the furniture. Creativity is like a child being a virtual spaceman!'

Creativity as a spur

Fiona Wright of Jacobs Engineering says: 'It is an idea in your head which you make real'. Helen Connolly of Kent County Council says that if things pop into your head you must pursue and articulate them and don't talk yourself out of it.

Simon Heath, Head of HR for A&N Media, defines creativity as 'being about thinking in a different way: independently while challenging the status quo. You must be brave, spontaneous but not foolhardy'.

For Alistair Summers of How2 Business Coaching, it is about the juxtaposition of things and ideas. He says: 'You need a spark that connects two semi related things to get an amazing picture out of it.'

In Focus

Interview with Kate Scally

Kate, Head of Consumer Strategy for A&N Media, when asked who the most creative person she knew was, immediately said 'myself', working in media and newspapers (A&N Media is the holding company for titles such as *The Mail, The Sunday Mail,* Mail Online and the *Metro* newspapers in the UK). She sees herself as at the vanguard of change in this market, which is changing at a rate like no other. Newspapers in general are looking at the demise of printed editions in the next few years. So, when interviewed she stated that creativity was really about expansive thinking, exploring ideas, new parameters, in a space conducive to ideas and solutions.

▶

◀

She firmly believes that space, both physical and metaphorical, is very important to creativity. It's all about the space and support for the 'what if' of future planning and finding a way to contemplate disconnected ideas to bring about creative solutions. She came up with four thinking styles that underlie the creative process: foraging, exploring, synthesizing and dissemination. I asked her permission to use these as outcome descriptions for the creative style questionnaire as they were wonderfully accurate. Kate is someone who completely understands the creative process and the part she plays.

Imagination

Martin Smith, Director at Miller Construction, says that for him it is 'using imagination to stamp your own identity on something,' while Liz Barlow of Kogan Page says that it is about uniqueness of vision.

Mihaela Alexandru, head of HR for Pilon Ltd, a training company, defines creativity as bringing innovative ideas to bear, to create something different which looks unique. Paul Fox of Babcock Marine says creativity resides in 'someone who is imaginative and is not scared to use their own ideas. It is an ability to look at things and see how they can be improved or modified'.

Efficiency of a code?

Rosemary McGinness, Global HR Director of William Grant and Sons, defines creativity as residing in 'Someone who can see things differently, who can keep an open mind to what is or is not possible.' But she thinks that in a work environment there is also the necessity of a practical application of creativity. Catch her interview later on, in Chapter 5.

For MD Ryan Hall of Nice Agency, 'delivering a practical solution that achieves what it needs to but at the same time delivers an inspirational product which provides the customer with sheer joy' is what true creativity is all about for him. 'The consumer should never realize or simply forget they purchased or paid money for their product because they enjoy it so much.' He was thinking of Apple at the time.

Sam Duncan-Brown, Head of Innovation for A&N Media, maintains that creativity is 'not just artistic'. It can also be in IT, for example 'the efficiency of a code'. So for him it is 'doing something different from where the boundaries were set before. It is the unexpected beyond the process'.

Margery McBain, CEO of Gravitate HR, says that a lot of people have ideas but they don't turn into anything and that, for her, is not creativity.

Speed, range and the big picture

It is the speed of ideas that is an important aspect of creativity for Shereen Muhyeddeen, Marketing Manager at Kogan Page publishers. It is 'someone with a distinct point of view, but able to express it in a number of different ways and can come up with new ideas fairly quickly'.

Stephanie Liston, Partner with Charles Russell LLP, says it is the 'ability to think broadly outside traditional delineation' and Sue O'Brien, CEO of Norman Broadbent Recruitment, defines creativity as 'seeing the big picture – the art of the possible not the probable. This takes you down a whole different path. It is the "what if" of creativity'.

Creativity as a response to limited resources

Maggie Berry, MD of Women in Technology (WIT), has a small membership organization so for her it is 'having cutting edge ideas and new solutions that must be delivered with little cost. That is creativity in action for most small businesses'.

Lindsay Baker, Head of HR for Stratus Technologies, says: 'The people that make the most out of limited resources are creative whether it is about people or money.' She told me about the time she was in her mid-20s running a coffee shop. She had no money for shop decoration so she asked customers to complete a limerick for the front of her menus and then put their input over the walls of the coffee shop.

It's about people

Occupational Psychologist Sue Mitchell feels that 'creativity can also be about bringing a way of thinking to a person. It can be a creative conversation like coaching for example which can be very creative'.

Iain Kennedy of Iain Kennedy Associates, a Scottish consultancy firm, defines creativity as 'being all about people coming together and becoming more than the sum of their parts'. Iain thinks this is such an enjoyable experience he can't understand why creativity in teams is not happening more often in organizations. And he claims it *really* is not happening as often as it should. To continue this theme, Kevin Beatty, CEO of A&N Media, underlines that 'creativity is nothing unless you can get people excited about it'.

Curiosity and sensational experience

Nancy Kim, Head of Sales with Theory fashion house, says 'my definition of creativity is the process and effective result of producing any and all things with aesthetic value. Everything from art to ideas, and all things concerned with a person's sensational experience'.

Sue Mitchell, Occupational Psychologist, again says 'there is something essential about curiosity and imagination. It can be in the artistic sense in terms of a visual or a picture but it is also an attitude and mind-set as well'. To her, it is about thinking: 'after thinking something through I have got something I want whether it be a solution to a problem or something aesthetic that does not currently exist'.

In Focus

Interview with Kate Downie

Born in North Carolina, Kate Downie studied at Grays School of Art in Aberdeen before travel and residencies took her to the United States, England, Amsterdam and Paris. Over the past two decades Kate has established herself as one of Scotland's most prominent artists.

When I interviewed Kate she told me that she views creativity as 'Fields of knowledge and relationships coming together for the creative idea.' Geographical dislocation acted as the grit of her artistic oyster. She said that moving around disrupts your vision and view of the world. Kate certainly lived in many places in the world as a result of her parents' jobs, so for her creativity was a kind of 'coping mechanism to make sense of the world'. She says: 'Curiosity is key to this process of creativity and also my ability to become bored easily. I had to make my own games and entertainment. I'm really not sure what is nurture or nature in all of this.'

The experts' view

Teresa Amabile

Teresa is a professor at the Harvard Business School. Her thoughts are clear in her article, 'Creativity and Innovation in Organizations'. She says:

... as humans we make up romantic tales about ourselves.
Falling in love is mysterious, thinking is mysterious ...
and so we create great words like 'creativity'.
Creativity is thinking: it just happens to be thinking that
leads to results that we think are great.

So Teresa's definition of creativity is 'the production of novel and useful ideas in any domain. In order for an idea or product to be considered creative it must be different from what has been done before'. Innovation on the other hand is 'the successful implementation of creative ideas within an organization'. So within her parameters, creativity is the starting point of innovation.

Dimis Michaelides

Dimis is a consultant and author, trainer and course designer, speaker and magician, who lives in Cyprus. He works in the areas of creativity and innovation, is Managing Director of Performa Consulting and a faculty member of the Cyprus International Institute of Management since 2009. He has been in the creativity business since birth it seems to me, so I was keen to hear about his definition, which is: imagining something new and making it happen.

When I interviewed him he was emphatic that there needs to be action involved for his definition of creativity. Overall he feels that leaders don't value creativity. They pay lip-service to it but would really like innovation without creativity as they fear the unusual. For him, creativity is multi-dimensional; it's about good teamwork and the time and space to have ideas. Some companies make it difficult to foster creativity. A banking group he worked with was entirely focused on one top man and it had a punitive blame culture. Dimis asks the question: can creativity exist in such a culture? He strongly feels that businesses need to have a way to approach risk and mistakes as fear stops ideas and kills creativity.

Companies need to work hard to have an environment that fosters creativity but also have a system that generates, collects and implements ideas. All of this is important for an effective outcome.

David Horth

David Horth is co-author of the award-winning *The Leader's Edge: Six creative competencies for navigating complex challenges*. He is a senior faculty member of the Center for Creative Leadership's Design Center based in the United States. For several successive years, *BusinessWeek* magazine has ranked the Center for Creative Leadership as number one for leadership development in its 'Executive education special report.' As well as delivering many programmes in which leadership and creativity are the major themes, David loves to coach executives to expand their creative horizons. Describing himself as an artist in training, David is a musician and poet who uses these gifts to coach and develop others.

I have met David many times at Creative Problem Solving Institute conferences. He firmly believes that creativity is about coming up with different ideas whether or not they are good or radical ... and utility should not be part of the equation. Ideas for him are ends in themselves.

David was born in England but has worked for many years in the United States, which he thinks is better than other nations at creativity. People there have a 'get up and go' mentality. The whole total quality movement was started in the United States but there still remains – even there – an advanced state of lip-service about creativity. David emphasized that there is a myth about the equation of more people + more money = more creativity. Not all companies 'get it' as they are not all like Google with a staff allowance of thinking time each week. I asked him, what is the one thing that organizations could do that would make the most difference? His reply:

Promote a few people who are creative. It is a symbolic way of shaking up the culture as everyone notices who has been advanced. That in turn leads to others modelling the behaviour. Education about the creative process is important and of course the fact that we are all creative.

Steps to creativity at work

✩   Think about your definition of creativity at work.
Review the definitions above and discover where your
own ideas fit.

✩   As a result of reading this chapter, might you broaden
your definition to include ideas that you could have about
your work?

✩   Did your definition of creativity perhaps hold you back
from thinking that you are creative? Was it too narrow?
Creativity is about new ideas in any domain.

Who are creative heroes at work?

I asked my 100 one-to-one interview group who were the most creative people they knew. I was interested to know if they saw the workplace as a natural habitat for creative heroes or if like me they viewed creativity as residing in the arts.

Artists and designers

The overwhelming response was that the most creative people they mentioned were artists or designers they had met or were in the family. It was interesting how many of this group did have artistic friends and relatives. Six degrees of separation!

Daniel Taylor of A&N Media cited his brother-in-law Raymond Henshaw as the most creative person he knew. Raymond produces large screen prints and has installed peace murals on gable ends in Belfast. Francisco Negrin, opera director, suggested Peter Sellers. Francisco had met him at lunch and noticed that Sellers was constantly creating or talking about creating. He was a man who saw endless possibilities; wonderful to behold but exhausting to be with. Liz Barlow of Kogan Page remembered her university lecturer Patricia Wooldridge and her poetry. Her poems moved in ways that took Liz by surprise. Louisa Martin of Cuttle Construction thought that her friend Scott who is a cobbler is the ultimate creative for her in the way he draws and creates shoes and boots.

Mike McEwan of Mike McEwan Ltd mentioned his son who left computer science to join a comedy troop doing improvisation work with audiences. Matthew Parnell's mother designed games for children with learning difficulties and Paul Heath's brother is a composer. They are both with Babcock Engineering.

Stephanie Liston, partner with Charles Russell LLP, described Peter York, who generated the term 'Sloan Ranger', as an 'artist' with words and the most creative person she knows. Susan Avarde, head of Global Branding at Citigroup, finds Mario Prada the most inventive person she knows and also Sophia Coppola the film maker.

Nancy Kim, a designer for the Theory fashion label, has Rei Kawakubo, creator and designer of Comme des Garçons as her creative idol. Rei was a leader in the avant garde fashion wave of the 1980s and the focus of her brand is 'to create what has never been created before'.

Kate Downie, artist, mentioned during interview that Angela Castro, a Brazilian clown, is the most creative person she has met in her experience and she works with many ... creative people that is, not clowns.

Jane Macleod, head of the legal department for The Phoenix Group, the UK's largest closed life and pension fund consolidator, felt that creativity had a pejorative connotation in her business, with echoes of the Barclays Bank LIBOR scandal still reverberating. So creativity for her is for those with an artistic bent.

The myth that creativity is the domain of art and artists is alive and well. More than 70 per cent of my interviewees mentioned artists, designers, poets, composers, film makers, writers, comedians and ... clowns as the most creative people they knew. However, some business examples did appear. Two business-oriented responses included Steve Jobs as the most creative and the least creative person of their acquaintance. Alistair Summers of How2 Business Coaching admired Steve Jobs' ability to take complex technology and turn it into something elegant that was adored by customers. Ashley Pover, CEO of Met Zurich, felt however that Steve Jobs was tyrannical in his leadership style, allowing only his own creativity to thrive thereby excluding other members of staff. Call me old-fashioned but it did seem to work.

Ashley felt that he himself had been rather creative when he was in the Army. He noticed that his fellow soldiers spent their pay packet in the first week and then had nothing left for the other three. He was more conservative with his cash, spending it slowly and wisely, so he started lending out money to his colleagues with a small percentage return. Banks wouldn't give soldiers loans as their earnings were low, so he was the only help in town. He says it was a win-win. He made some extra money and they survived till another pay day.

A creative hero at work mentioned by members of my own team is Howard Schultz, founder of Starbucks.

In Focus

No silver bullet – Howard Schultz, founder of Starbucks

Howard Schultz founded Starbucks after a visit to Italy where he was introduced to 'proper coffee', not the dilution that was previously on offer in the United States. Bringing good coffee to the United States is almost sufficient in itself to put him in the 'creative hero' category. I heard Howard Schultz speak in London recently and he mentioned that over the last five years he had been looking for a silver bullet that would single-handedly restore the fortunes of his struggling empire.

He saw his company's recent tribulations as a case study in what can happen to a business that uses growth as a strategy rather than a tactic. For the better part of 15 years, he explains, from 1992 to 2006:

▶

◀

practically everything the company did produced a level of success and adulation. Yet Starbucks' consistent successes distorted its managers' view of their own creativity. If Frappuccino is a hot category and you introduce a new flavour, and it moves the needle a lot, the organization comes to believe, 'that was a great thing we did'. And it imprints a feeling of, 'That was innovation. But that's not innovation. In fact, it's laziness'.

The tweaking of a product, by his criteria, involves little in the way of risk taking or long-range vision. And that was the problem with the old Starbucks.

So he went back to basics and for a day closed all the stores in the United States and retrained the baristas in how to make a great cup of coffee. The stock price fell. The newspapers of course had a field day – 'Starbucks not knowing how to make coffee!' but it paid off in the end. He wanted his offering to be about quality not just about the quantity of coffee sold.

Now Howard Schultz has plans for redesigned stores, investments in innovative coffee machines, an expansion of its digital networks and rewards programmes, and he is striving for every branch to be more versatile.

So, no silver bullet, just great coffee and creative diversification.

Sue O'Brien of Norman Broadbent Recruitment had Nick Robertson of ASOS, the online fashion site, at the top of her list of most creative people. She feels that he has a vision of what is possible and pushes back boundaries to get there. ASOS now dominates the online fashion business.

Helen Connolly of Kent Council mentioned a fellow teaching colleague from Australia who was very creative in her teaching methods. She split her class into those with blue eyes and those with brown ones. The blue eyes won rewards and sat at the top of the class. She watched the behaviour of the children change as the blue eyes started 'lording it' over the brown eyes. After a day she changed the groups around. It was payback time for the brown eyes. They dominated the blue eyes, settling scores over arguments fostered the previous day. What great learning for children about lack of inclusion and suppression and in a way that books and traditional teaching methods would simply not supply. This is true creativity at work (and of course she got permission from the parents about the project, in case anyone was worrying).

A very few responses focused on the synergy of 'art' and business.

In Focus

Sweating the detail is creative

Billy Differ, who works as Operations Director for Delfont Mackintosh theatres in London, immediately suggested Sir Cameron Mackintosh as the most creative person he had ever met. He is visually creative while at the same time has an ability to absorb information and problem solve. Impresario Sir Cameron pipped Sir Andrew Lloyd Weber as *Stage* magazine's most influential person in British theatre. He is particularly famous for his stagings of 'Les Miserables', 'Phantom of the Opera' and 'Miss Saigon'.

When he was refurbishing The Prince of Wales Theatre he immediately saw that a wall had to be taken down not just for the aesthetics of the place but also for customer traffic flow. Construction guys demurred in that way they have: 'Supporting wall – can't be done gov', all comments ignored by Mackintosh and he was right. The space improved and the theatre remained standing.

Mackintosh has an exceptional eye for detail, according to Billy, which is renowned in the entertainment business. He hated the sanitary bins in the women's toilets. They reminded him of some utilitarian hospital equipment not nearly luxurious enough for his theatre toilets. So he got gold prototypes made to suit the ambience of the Queens Theatre ... all of this while he was making the film of 'Les Miserables'.

So there was Billy traversing London with a series of sanitary bins for Mackintosh to view – all grist to the mill of an Operations Director but difficult to put on his CV.

Susan Hart, Dean of Strathclyde Business School, felt that a friend of hers who is a trainer of play workers for children was her creative hero. She manages to balance the regulatory requirements on working with kids with creating exciting games. But it doesn't stop there, as she runs children's parties for McDonald's restaurants and has acquired Lottery funding to institute play facilities for the Birmingham area – she manages to combine creativity with a business head.

So, when asked, the majority of our sample, despite knowing that the project was about creativity at work, did not immediately suggest business-related creativity. The arts proliferated. What does it take for us to see the world of work as the target of creativity? And if employees, directors and CEOs don't see their workplace as a space for creativity and their role as fostering it, how can we expect there to be new ideas, new directions and true innovation in business?

What I *did* learn was that despite thinking that creativity was the preserve of the artistic, my interviewees still had ideas at work but didn't rate that as being creative. If we adhere to the definition by the researchers in the field, their contributions quite definitely are creative. Also, from the creative heroes that were mentioned at work, we discovered that creativity can be in the detail as well as returning to a quality product and engaging in true diversification.

Steps to creativity at work

 Reflect on your choice of the most creative person you know.

 What are their attributes?

 If your chosen creative person is in the arts, think about anyone at work who is creative or uses creative solutions. What could be learnt from thinking about their skills and behaviour? How could you put these attributes into practice?

How creative do you think you are?

People in my interview group rated themselves on a creativity scale of one to 10 without being asked to do so; the lowest rated themselves as a four and the highest an eight. Rate yourself now before reading more. It was noticeable that those who had thought creativity was 'about the arts' were more likely to downgrade their own powers of creativity saying, 'I'm not creatively artistic but ...'.

Nancy Kim, head of sales for Theory, says: 'I am not a person that creates but I think I can take and absorb a product or idea and translate it for others. I can also make connections between people, brands, merchandise and how they all work in conjunction with the world we live in.'

Louisa Martin, Cuttle Construction, says: 'I don't feel particularly creative as I don't really have any artistic flair or "out there" ideas, nor do I turn them into anything substantial should I have one. I just work on solutions to problems.'

Constrained by work or education

Lindsay Baker of Stratus says that it really depends on the context. When she was running her own business, she had to be very creative because she had to keep the business going. 'At work you are constrained by the organization that you work for. There is a creative person that wants to get out but, because of my job, I am probably about a five or six.'

Fiona Wright of Jacobs thinks: 'Outside work I am quite creative because I enjoy creating ideas and will try making things at home.' At work she is limited as she is the PA to the Vice President. She can take the raw material that people produce in presentations and then reformat it. But she is constrained by what she can do.

Alistair Summers of How2 Business Coaching gave himself seven out of 10: 'I was not brought up like that. The education system does not enable you to think in a creative way.'

In Focus

There's always someone else more creative!

Francisco Negrin was born in Mexico and is now based in Barcelona. Over the past 20 years his creative genius, particularly in opera direction, has earned him considerable public success and international acclaim. Many of his opera productions have been revived many times, and several have been filmed for television ('Una Cosa Rara', 'Venus', 'Les Contes d'Hoffmann,' two different 'Giulio Cesare' and 'Norma'). I have always known that Francisco has a keen interest in teaching and he has devised an innovative series of master classes for singers at the Opera Academy in Copenhagen. He also pursues his interest in other media, feature films and editing several shorts and music videos. He recently e-mailed me to tell me that he now has earned an entry in Wikipedia. He was so proud.

However, Francisco rated himself only an eight out of 10 for creativity. 'I am not a visionary' he says. He admires the totally new. 'I am just a synthesizer of what I see and then transferring it to the stage.' Francisco describes himself as an educator. He educates his

▶

audience by taking them by the hand and leading them through his vision of the piece of work. In this way, he says, 'I don't create from scratch.' When I suggested that what he described was the very essence of creativity he was unmoved: 'I'm certainly neither Einstein nor Peter Brook.'

So there's always someone more creative even if you are a celebrated opera director!

Ryan Hall, MD of Nice Agency, also claims he is only averagely creative. Ryan feels that in his role as MD he has to challenge the more creative people around him. He sees solutions and through being disruptive can help challenge those who are creative to achieve better solutions. He surrounds himself with people who are more proficient at being creative than him. But is that not creativity in itself?

Intermittent creativity

Consultant Diane Gordon awards herself five out of 10. She has 'sparks of creativity but then nothing for a really long time', like Faye Melly of KPMG who only on good days can be 'fairly creative'.

I'm just ...

Helen Connolly of Kent County Council UK says: 'I'm not creative.' She remembers as a child continually unpicking her hand-made apron at domestic science class. This has clearly scarred her for life as she says she is not creative at all, 'just an ideas' person.

Hayley Fry of the Federation of Master Builders only allows herself a small amount of creativity – four out of 10. And yet she has completely transformed the FMB training offering and instituted a Green Deal Programme with accreditation for builders.

Kevin Beatty, CEO at A&N Media, says he is just creative in the way he gets things done.

I'm really, really not creative

Lisa Heneghan of KPMG says: 'In business I am action-oriented. There is no time to be creative in my working environment.'

Stephanie Liston, Partner at Charles Russell, says: 'I'm a lawyer for goodness sake!'

Steps to creativity at work

✰ Do you underestimate your creativity like our sample here?

✰ Creativity is not the preserve of the arts. Having ideas at work and solving problems is justifiable creativity.

✰ Learn about your own creative style in the next chapter.

Your creative style

David Horth claimed that we are all creative, so I produced a creative style questionnaire based upon research carried out by Min Basadur in the United States. I really wanted to prove to my group of interviewees that they were indeed creative and to highlight their particular contribution to creativity. Complete the questionnaire yourself and then add your scores to Figure 4.1.

Questionnaire

Figure 4.1 Creative style questionnaire

	Column 1	Column 2	Column 3	Column 4
1.	☐ Doing	☐ Childlike	☐ Observing	☐ Realistic
2.	☐ Experiencing	☐ Diversifying	☐ Waiting	☐ Consolidating
3.	☐ Trial and Error	☐ Alternatives	☐ Pondering	☐ Evaluating
4.	☐ Action	☐ Divergence	☐ Abstraction	☐ Convergence

Figure 4.1 *continued*

	Column 1	Column 2	Column 3	Column 4
5.	☐ Direct	☐ Possibilities	☐ Conceptual	☐ Practical
6.	☐ Involved	☐ Changing perspectives	☐ Theoretical	☐ Focusing
7.	☐ Implementing	☐ Visualizing	☐ Describing	☐ Pinpointing
8.	☐ Hands-on	☐ Future oriented	☐ Research	☐ Detail oriented
9.	☐ Physical	☐ Creating options	☐ Psychological	☐ Making decisions
10.	☐ Practising	☐ Transforming	☐ Thinking	☐ Choosing
11.	☐ Handling	☐ Speculating	☐ Contemplating	☐ Judging
12.	☐ Contacting	☐ Innovating	☐ Reflecting	☐ Ensuring
Total Scores	☐ +	☐ +	☐ +	☐ = 120

This questionnaire is designed to describe your way of problem solving and being creative. It is not about what might be right or wrong or indeed evaluation whatsoever. Different styles are equally good.

Instructions

Start filling each row horizontally, by rating the adjectives and descriptions from 1 to 4, where 4 is best and 1 is least. Make sure to assign a different number to each of the four words or phrases in each row from left to right. For example ☐2 Positive ☐3 Analytical ☐1 Decisive ☐4 Open minded

How you work out your profile

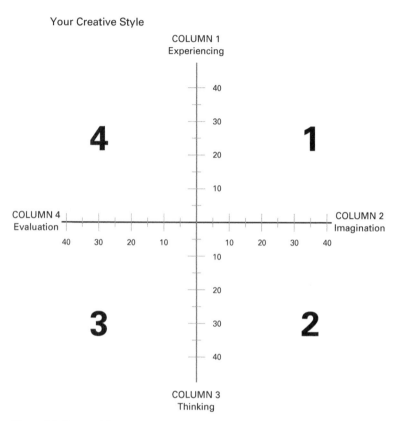

Figure 4.1 Your profile

First, plot your scores from columns 1, 2, 3 and 4 on each corresponding axis shown in Figure 4.1, then connect the four points with four lines. *Your profile is your own unique blend of the four quadrants. It's your 'shape' that counts.* The quadrant in which your profile is most dominant indicates your strongest orientation. The other quadrants represent secondary styles.

Interpretation: the four creative styles

Table 4.2 The four creative styles

4. Disseminator	1. Forager
<ul><li>Disseminates activities around ideas</li><li>Gets things done</li><li>Adapts to make things work</li><li>Will discard theory if not fitting the facts</li><li>Tries things out rather than thinking things through</li><li>Takes risks</li><li>Willing to try many approaches till one is completely acceptable</li><li>Enthusiastic with people but impatient for action</li><li>Focuses on getting buy-in and action</li></ul>	<ul><li>Forages for information</li><li>Initiates, gets things started</li><li>Loves discussion and listening to others' ideas</li><li>Imagines many possibilities and sees opportunities</li><li>Looks at situations from different perspectives</li><li>Comfortable with ambiguity</li><li>Willing to let others go into details not them</li><li>Focuses on problem finding and fact finding</li></ul>
3. Synthesizer	**2. Explorer**
<ul><li>Synthesizes concepts into practical solutions</li><li>Can pinpoint glitches and errors</li><li>Selects the best solutions to problems</li><li>Dislikes ambiguity</li><li>Likes to focus on specific problems</li><li>Is thorough and objective</li><li>Evaluates ideas and information</li><li>Focuses on selecting ideas and planning what to do with them</li></ul>	<ul><li>Explores new ideas and opportunities</li><li>Takes unrelated ideas and facts and integrates them</li><li>Likes to understand a situation fully</li><li>Wants any theory to be well validated</li><li>Enjoys doing things their way</li><li>Appreciates ideas over action</li><li>Visualizes the big picture</li><li>Focuses on problem definition and idea finding</li></ul>

It is important to know your own style as that knowledge sets you free; see Table 4.2. You are at last able to call yourself creative as indeed we all are, and can utilize that knowledge for the greater good in whatever you do. It really means that you do not have to be anyone else but yourself. In the same way as the leadership style questionnaire that featured in my last book, *Confidence at Work*, enabled you to know your strengths and capitalize on them, so does knowing your creative style. It adds to your portfolio of knowledge, that picture of yourself.

What creativity research reveals is that everyone is a blend of preferences. Different personality types, jobs or functions within an organization may favour different creative styles. You can of course be skilled in all four styles. What is more usual, however, is that you have a preference for one or two styles, with the rest having a lesser impact. Our courageous group of interviewees completed 'Your creative style' and I will share some of their results with you.

Ashley Pover, the CEO of Met Zurich, is a Forager and he mentioned previously that he was always looking for new angles and ideas to engage with clients. Another Forager is Anne Fergusson, director at PWC. She sees herself as an ambassador for the company and forages for people. She creatively brings disparate people together to enable projects to flourish and clients to be helped.

Kate Scally is an off-the-scale Explorer, constantly thinking about new ways of doing things and having an overabundance of ideas. Sometimes, she confided, she has so many that she sees people looking at her oddly. Ideas are her strength and the unexpected her currency. Every organization needs at least one.

Francisco Negrin, Opera Director, is a Synthesizer. He is a good teacher, which is essential when communicating his vision to singers. As a true Synthesizer he quickly identifies priorities and is excellent at seeing glitches in systems. He dislikes computer manuals or indeed any manual for a machine. He can cut through the verbiage and offer a simpler version in minutes. He normally has a queue of people at his door wanting help with their computers and iPads.

Ryan Hall, MD of Nice Agency, is a Disseminator. The clue to his style was when he said that he kept his creative staff in check and seeks solutions. Ryan wants outcomes for clients and challenges his team to focus on that and not just the ideas themselves. They are strong divergers and he is a converger.

In Focus

Susan Avarde – 'Thank You'

Susan is Head of Global Branding for Citigroup, based in New York, where I interviewed her. She oversees the brand in 140 countries. At any given time Susan may have 30 different brand programmes in development. She was an attendee at the 2011 White House luncheon hosted by Michelle Obama honouring the Best American Designers.

In 2004 she led the team to create a customer rewards programme for Citi, which was launched five years ago. It was very successful and has been lauded as one of the most original in the industry. She told me that many names had been proposed for this programme including 'Pizazz' and 'Gherkin'. She eventually cut across all of these ideas, suggesting 'Thank You' as the name. She felt it had to be simple, not clever, and really deliver 'what it said on the tin'.

Having not previously described herself as creative but as a coordinator and supporter of other creatives, she was delighted to discover that she was a Disseminator. She is predisposed to action and cutting across discussion to suggest a name so that everyone could move on is often a Disseminator's role, especially when you head up the team!

Creativity research

Researchers into creativity like Min Basadur, Professor Emeritus at McMaster University, Hamilton, Ontario, states that teams with a heterogeneous mix of creative styles, significantly out-perform teams with a homogeneous mix in innovative work. But in contrast, members of homogeneous groups experience more satisfaction working with their like-minded teammates.

So a diverse team, with all creative styles represented, will perform better. However, that team may have an uncomfortable time coming to agreement about how to problem solve. Explorers who love concepts, brainstorming and ideas can be at odds with Disseminators who just want the job done and finished. Synthesizers want everything to be correct and focused and so they also may be irritated by the Explorer. Meanwhile the Explorer is wondering why the rest don't just love 'blue sky thinking' or thinking 'out of the box' in the way that he or she does. Foragers on the other hand love seeing opportunities in everything and have a constant flow of ideas about all the directions the business could go, but since they really don't like the detail, they tend to initiate ideas but don't close them, which might anger others.

Of course understanding where everyone fits in a team helps to reduce confusion and conflict, allowing team members to play to their individual strengths. It gets back to selection and the human tendency to have people around us who are like us, when what functions best is diversity. Even better is when you all know who is best at what.

I remember working with a newly formed team of engineers who apparently roundly hated each other. I had no idea about this enmity but noticed there was some silence initially as I started a series of leadership seminars with them. As we progressed through discovering leadership styles, team types and creativity styles, they began to understand why a 'nit picking' colleague was important to the team and the woman who had 'grandiose ideas' – their words – was wonderful at getting them to think more expansively. Conflict diminished and teamwork increased with a profound effect on performance: it was four times what had been expected of them that year.

The arrows

So what do the arrows mean in Figure 4.2? There is an ideal process when a team wants to be creative in order to solve a problem or come up with new ideas at work. The optimum way to pursue this is to start foraging for ideas, for example from competitors, customers or indeed abroad. The next stage is to explore different ideas and options that might work for your organization. These would be synthesized and evaluated for

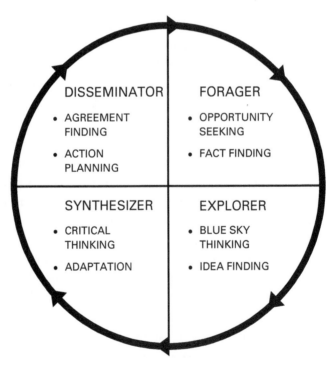

Figure 4.2 The creative process

workability before getting buy-in for dissemination. Miss any of these steps and solutions are either too banal or simple reworkings of the old, tried and tested ones or, even worse, solutions to the wrong problems. So foraging starts the process and ends with dissemination, ready to start all over again with another issue. Part IV of this book will suggest an easy process to use in teams.

Divergence and convergence

When problem solving or making decisions, you can use two processes: divergence and convergence, and they have quite different thinking methods.

Divergence

When you need to explore and find new things, you use divergent approaches. This is a process of looking for options, new ideas and so on. Some people prefer diverging, as it means the potential of a wrong decision is never reached. They just keep diverging.

An important first step of divergent thinking is to be open. As a cognitive state, it involves suspending judgement and deliberately opening yourself up to new thoughts and ideas. If you are seeking to change someone else's mind, opening them up to the possibility of new thoughts is often an important first step. Creative generation of ideas is a classic divergent activity, although it is not the only one. In creative sessions, ideas are suggested without judgement or thought about which works best.

Convergence

Convergence is the opposite of divergence. When you are thinking in a convergent manner you are seeking a conclusion, an answer, and closure on the topic in question. People who rapidly seek convergence often have a preference for the structure of judgement, evaluation and action. Conflict can happen in groups when one person is diverging and another is converging. The result is that they are going in different directions at the same time, which is never a good thing.

I have just returned from Chicago where I was working with senior movers and shakers in economic development. They completed the creative style questionnaire and the results were fascinating: only three out of 90 attendees were Explorers. The rest were found to be Foragers, Synthesizers or Disseminators. With few Explorers in a sector, that kind of 'blue sky' creativity will be limited and that profession will be less impactful as a result.

You need all four creativity styles to get the most out of ideas and problem solving in an organization. Foragers and Explorers are the divergent thinkers in a team. They open areas up for discussion and enjoy unchartered territory. Synthesizers and Disseminators are keen to converge, which means they want closure; they also want a plan.

I have noticed in many companies today that there is a tendency for teams to forage for data with surveys and research and will make decisions on the basis of that information. So Foraging goes straight to Dissemination – these people are missing out on the vital ingredient of seeking other options, other views and looking at the 'what if' of unusual ideas and evaluating them. They are missing out on half the process and sadly will get half a result.

An example comes to mind. I was working with the HR department at Arthur Anderson, the now defunct accountancy firm. It was going to make people redundant as part of a cost-cutting exercise being initiated throughout the firm. Managers discussed all the ingredients of the situation and were going to proceed to the best and most humane way of carrying out the downsizing – an example of 'foraging straight to dissemination'. Then one of the managers mentioned how short term she thought the redundancies were, as they would have to rehire when the various year-ends happened at different times around the world. That stopped the group in their tracks. Someone was then tasked to check on this by looking at international diaries and costs. The outcome was that this manager's observation led to an ingenious programme of peripatetic accountants flying around the world to help out at year-ends. No one was made redundant. Without a bit of creative thinking that option would never have been considered.

Teams and creative styles

Let's look at a real example of a top team. I have called them 'Distribution and Co'. The CEO and Finance Director are Disseminators and there are three Explorers but only one Synthesizer and no first choice Foragers (see Figure 4.3). So no one is formally out looking for opportunities. Perhaps they are relying on ideas coming internally from the team and organization, but who is taking responsibility for that process? They may be inundated with ideas that are irrelevant. So the Explorers who are more junior in the team could be frustrated, starved of suitable new things to discuss and pursue. There is only one Synthesizer and she is much younger than the others so if she wants to criticize, evaluate or adapt suggestions she will have to be very confident about putting her point across. So this team should hire someone to generate and coordinate opportunities for change and also another Synthesizer to evaluate and put ideas to practical purpose. Two senior Disseminators could mean that the urge for action is so strong that they may override the input from the rest of the group and miss out on creative ideas and opportunities for change.

Let's look at another real team of engineers (with an unreal name) in 'The Slick Engineering Company'. There are eight in this team who are all at the same level and work together on

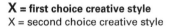

X = first choice creative style
X = second choice creative style

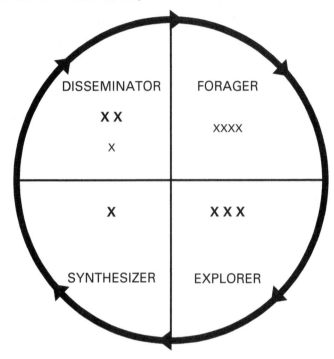

Figure 4.3 Distribution and Co

a variety of projects; see Figure 4.4. They are all young and very intelligent.

It doesn't take a trained observer to notice that there is more activity on the top level of the creative style team results than the bottom. So much Foraging going on with lots of opportunities, new ideas probably about the current project, possibly more data-oriented as a result of research. There are two first choice Explorers and one Synthesizer so unless these team members are outspoken a risk in this team is that you get the Forager/ Disseminator coalition without considering the more creative options with practical implementation. Many missed opportunities perhaps.

X = first choice creative style
X = second choice creative style

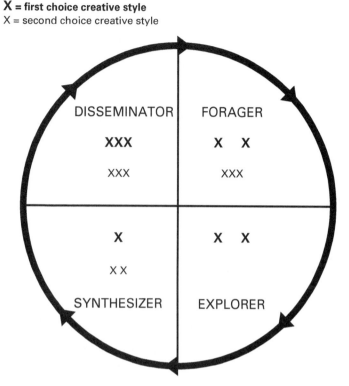

Figure 4.4 The Slick Engineering Company

Let me give you a practical example of how this works or rather, doesn't. The story is about a family business. The Moto Trading Company. It sold cars online. The company had been in the market a long time and dealt with large dealerships, but to grow the business it needed access to more cars and that meant involving smaller dealers. It did the research and when the managers looked at the figures they couldn't see how they could make a profit because to make all these connections was seen as too labour-intensive and expensive. So they sold the business. This is a good example of Foraging for information and then proceeding straight to Dissemination. There just might have been another way but it was never explored. Perhaps this was the best decision but it was simply premature to foreclose on the basis of discovered facts alone.

So you need all four quadrants filled to produce a creatively balanced team. Do companies actively hire for creativity? Are candidates routinely assessed for their creative styles? No they are not.

I noticed a posting on an HR Linkedin Group of which I am a member. An HR professional had asked the group how they would assess for a creative hire. The resounding answer was that you just know a creative when you see them. Really, but what kind?

Steps to creativity at work

 Discover your own creative style.

 Ensure that those around you discover their style.

 Use the questionnaire to hire for the gaps in creative style for your teams.

Creativity in organizations

Let's leave individuals and teams and look at the organizations represented in our interview group. In this chapter you will discover how they go about their creative endeavours and find examples of creativity at work.

I am really interested to know how integrated creativity is in organizations. Does it happen sporadically or as part of every meeting? What process is being used and what tools and techniques? And of course what is happening creatively in the organizations represented in our sample? The results from our sample of 100 interviewees on the creative processes they use are:

Brainstorming	14
Mind Mapping	6
A creative process	3
Team debate	2
Six Thinking Hats	1
Getting young people involved	1
Open culture of debate	1
Total	28

Twenty-eight people out of 100 in our one-to-one interview sample used some tool or technique to generate creative ideas in their teams, which represents of course 28 per cent of the group. However, only three people/per cent used a creative process to solve problems or generate creative ideas. Of the three who used a process, two were consultants and one an engineer. They would utilize their creative process two or three times a week. Those who brainstormed or Mind Mapped with their teams did so usually on a monthly basis.

The rest of the group, who did not utilize any process, mentioned meeting only quarterly or yearly to discuss future ideas and planning. The latter does not seem to me to constitute the integration of creativity in the workplace.

Creative tools

I thought it worthwhile to examine more closely the tools and techniques that the group of 28 used so that you could be encouraged to use creative tools at work too. The three common ones mentioned by the group were brainstorming, Mind Mapping and Six Thinking Hats.

Brainstorming

Brainstorming is a group creativity technique where efforts are made to find a solution for a specific problem by gathering a list of ideas spontaneously contributed by its members. The term was popularized by Alex Osborn in his 1953 book *Applied Imagination* (Read Books, 2011). The whole idea, Alex claimed, was that brainstorming is more effective than generating ideas by yourself as people can bounce their thinking off each other.

Brainstorming started when Osborn was frustrated by his employees' inability to develop creative ideas individually for ad campaigns. In response, he began hosting group-thinking sessions and discovered a significant improvement in the quality and quantity of ideas. Osborn claimed that two major principles contributed to the acquisition of ideas: deferring judgement and quantity not quality. He also had four general rules of brainstorming (see below) that aimed to reduce inhibitions among group members, stimulate ideas, and increase the overall creativity of the group. Later in the book we will explore why this is so necessary because of the way we think.

I had always felt slightly irritated by brainstorming in the past. Some poor sucker was at the flipchart writing down ideas that had to be dragged from a reluctant group. It was usually at the end of a meeting when everyone wanted to go to the bar or go home. When I first attended a Creative Problem Solving Institute Conference in Buffalo many years ago it was a revelation to me when I witnessed and then participated in 'proper' brainstorming.

Of course Buffalo University was home to Alex Osborn, the inventor of brainstorming in the 1940s. He collaborated with Sid Parnes to establish CEF – the Creative Education Foundation. Sid Parnes, in his book *Optimize the Magic of your Mind* (Bearly Ltd, 1997) contends that we live in a cultural cocoon in which we don't see the new and different. As he says, 'a child has oodles of imagination but no judgement; the adult has loads of judgement but loses imagination'. We all have the capacity for creativity but that ability is equally undermined by our habitual, knee-jerk thinking. Sid would have it that we are frightened by our ideas in case they are open to ridicule.

Brainstorming suggests suspending judgement to help the flow of ideas. This is of course challenging if you have had 20 to 40 years being critical and judgemental about yourself and others. So some training is required for groups to free up their imagination so that they can form new connections.

Some recent literature cites research that casts doubt on the utility of brainstorming and the positive reinforcement that surrounds the process. Jonah Lehrer, in his book *Imagination* (Canongate, 2012), cites a couple of studies, the first at Yale in 1958. It claims that more ideas, especially 'do-able ideas' are obtained by people working on their own. I certainly have never noticed that. When I have supplied one group with Post-It pads to work individually to come up with ideas, they are always surpassed by groups working together brainstorming. And 'do-able' ideas are not usually the best either. If you want to be truly creative it is much better to have wild ideas you can tame. However, groups do have to practise the tenets of brainstorming as this does not necessarily come naturally.

The next study Lehrer mentions was conducted in Berkeley by Charlan Nemeth, on the tenet of deferring judgement. One group were supportive of each other's ideas, the other critical. Apparently the critical group produced 25 per cent more ideas. She called this the 'debate' group. Now there's debate and there's debate. If scathing and undermining, I can't imagine ideas existing in that climate. I remember when I worked in television and was invited to a discussion about the televising of the Edinburgh Festival. No one was speaking up so I ventured an idea only for it to be shot down in flames and called stupid. It was the last idea I ever aired in that forum. The idea probably was foolish but the response certainly did not encourage me to have any more, thank you very much!

Note that brainstorming suggests *deferring* judgement, not that there should be no judgement at all. Critical faculties are in use as soon as you have a list of ideas and you want to choose the best to work on. Groups can be as critical as they want at this stage but without personal slights, as the ideas delivered are the outcomes of combined minds.

The suggestion that you would bring a group together to have them work separately on a problem or issue seems counterproductive to me. It just doesn't make sense. And the idea that you would criticize and judge the offerings from others and that would somehow encourage additional input again seems incomprehensible. It's like seeing some small green shoots, trampling over them in large boots and expecting them to survive.

If we take a look at Teresa Amabile's 2012 research in *The Progress Principle* (Harvard Business School Press, 2011) it provides some insight. From hundreds of thousands of diary entries she discovered that with a background of positive support her research group were consistently and significantly more creative for up to two days after the good feedback. What of course might be happening is individual difference. Extraverts prefer the group set up and introverts the individual. (Myers Briggs and H J Eysenck have revealed the difference in orientation of extraverts and introverts.) Women also look to relationships to problem solve. They are three times more likely than men to seek out interpersonal solutions from a GP or therapist. So introverted men might find brainstorming a challenge unless a skilled leader can use a variety of techniques to overcome their reluctance and include their ideas. Brainstorming works, ok.

The four rules

1 *Focus on quantity:* This rule is a means of enhancing divergent production of ideas, aiming to facilitate problem solving through the maxim 'quantity breeds quality'. The assumption is that the greater the number of ideas generated, the greater the chance of producing a radical and effective solution.

2 *No criticism:* In brainstorming, criticism of ideas generated should be put on hold. Instead, participants should focus on extending or adding to ideas, reserving criticism for a later evaluation stage of the process. By suspending judgement, participants will feel free to come up with more 'off the wall' ideas.

3 *Reward unusual ideas:* To get a long list of ideas, unusual ideas are welcomed. They can be generated by looking from new perspectives and suspending assumptions. These new ways of thinking can provide better solutions.

4 *Combine and improve ideas:* Good ideas may be combined to form a single, even better, good idea. This process is often called 'piggybacking' as group members add to others' ideas as they are written down or shouted out.

The main proposition about brainstorming is that it is fun and creates the energy to generate new things.

Mind Mapping

Mind Maps can help an individual or team speedily identify the overall concept and structure of a subject because you can see the way that pieces of information fit together. Mind Mapping can also help you to remember information as it is in a format that you find easy to recall and quick to revise. Wonderful for presentations! I am not sure that I would have been able to speak at so many conferences and seminars if Mind Mapping had been unavailable as a tool.

Mind Maps were popularized by Tony Buzan and because they are more compact than conventional notes, often taking up

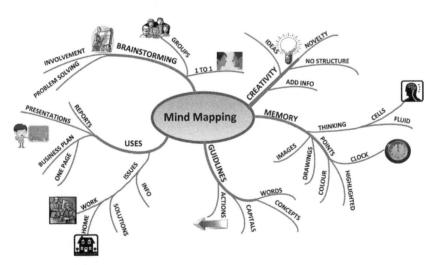

Figure 5.1 Mind Mapping

one side of paper, you can make associations more easily, and generate new ideas. If you find out more information after you have drawn a Mind Map, then you can just add it with little disruption. When I think back to working in a linear structure with arrows all over the place, adding new ideas as they came to me, I realized it was a mess leading to befuddled thinking.

In addition to this, Mind Mapping helps you to break down large projects or topics into manageable chunks, so that you can plan effectively without getting overwhelmed and without forgetting something important. I have used Mind Mapping increasingly for business plans. At every meeting you can produce the map and add to it if necessary. It's all on one page. Simple.

Guidelines for Mind Mapping

- Put the title in the centre.
- Use capitals – you can see them more easily.
- Use lines for information connected to the centre.
- Use only one or two words along the lines.
- Use colour to identify sections and aid memory.
- Keep your mind free of structure.

Six Thinking Hats

The premise of the Six Thinking Hats method is that the human brain thinks in a number of distinct ways. Edward De Bono (Penguin, 2009) identified six different modes. Since the hats don't represent natural ways of thinking, each hat must be used for a short time only. Many people (including me) feel that using the hats – even metaphorically – is unnatural, uncomfortable or even counter-productive to creativity and spontaneity. However, it is an interesting concept that explores the utility of certain thinking styles for different sets of circumstances. It just seems like an accountant's take on thinking for me, a little too segmented and structured. But that probably tells you more about me than De Bono.

The Six Thinking Hats process attempts to introduce parallel thinking when in a group. Ordinary, unstructured thinking tends to be unfocused; the thinker leaps from critical thinking to neutrality to optimism, etc without structure or strategy. When thinking in a group these individual strategies will not tend to converge and so discussion will also not converge. This can lead to very destructive meetings. The Hats allow this to be avoided so that everyone considers the problems, benefits or facts together, thus reducing distractions and supporting cross-fertilization of thought. This is achieved because everyone puts on one hat (eg, the white hat) then they all put on the next hat together. So everyone thinks in the same way at the same time. The only exception is the facilitator, who keeps on the blue hat of leadership all the time to make sure things progress effectively.

Six different thinking styles and associated colours

- *Information* (white) – considering purely what information is available; what are the facts?

- *Emotions* (red) – intuitive or instinctive gut reactions or statements of emotional feeling.

- *Discernment* (black) – logic applied to identifying reasons to be cautious and conservative.

- *Optimistic response* (yellow) – logic applied to identifying benefits, seeking harmony.

- *Creativity* (green) – statements of provocation and investigation, seeing where a thought leads.

- *Leadership* (blue) – outward-looking, trail-blazing hat.

Some people swear by it. For example when I interviewed David Hogarth, FD at Deutsche Bank, he had a list of green thoughts on the white board in his office. He uses it to great effect with his team.

Examples of creativity in the workplace

Despite 70 per cent of our sample of 100 believing that creativity resides in art and not the workplace, they did come up with many examples of projects that pushed back boundaries or were creatively new.

Day-to-day examples of creativity at work

I spoke to Dorothy Fenwick in Edinburgh who has had a career spanning some 30 years in Scotland and the UK, mostly with Scottish public sector agencies at director level. She now has her own corporate communications company and is on the board of Visit Scotland, which spearheads tourism for Scotland. She told me about Visit Scotland's initiative, which has 100 groups of businesses around Scotland to encourage them to be part of a common set of targets for tourism. She and others on the board wanted to help not just the numerous bed and breakfast establishments but everything that pertained to communities through the businesses. This is a fresh vision that has at its heart the view that developing business develops communities and therefore tourism.

Helen Connolly of Kent County Council UK talked to me about the Pathways Programme Online that has been developed by her department. Anyone wanting to work with the council can submit or declare an interest in job opportunities by applying online and submitting their CV where it will be matched against available jobs. This showed a creative use of technology for ease and speed.

Kim Roditi of A&N Media is very proud of product managing a new fashion website launched recently for women aged 16 to 35 (so not for me then!) It taps into social media, and generates revenue from advertising.

Lisa Heneghan, Partner at KPMG, told me of a time when the firm didn't pursue its normal engagement with clients. It was tasked with helping its clients deal with Personal Protection Insurance (PPI) mis-selling claims. The firm would usually send in consultants charging the usual daily rate; this time it created a remediation capability to process all claims. This was a speedier, more client-focused solution and ended up providing KPMG with a huge revenue stream. A truly creative win/win.

Liz Barlow, editor at Kogan Page, suggested a day-to-day example for her. She is constantly looking at competing books and asking 'How can I produce something better?' She has started to use a more systematic approach – listing any faults and forming an 'ideal' of what she wants.

Margery McBain, CEO of Gravitate HR, had been working on a complex case that involved many different employees and different relationships and dispute issues with the client. They had been working with the directors to resolve the issues. It then became apparent that the directors were part of the problem and so the process that they had in mind via discussion was not going to work. Instead they had to find a way to consider alternative methods of dispute resolution. They had to be quite creative in gaining their trust so the client would be open to the company's ideas of new thinking. They were successful in doing so.

Scott Miller, Director at Badenoch and Clark, has introduced a unique reward strategy to allow some of his consultants to focus on their strengths in business delivery rather than just focus on business development. He is trialling this right now.

Rosemary McGinness 'A literal phoenix from the ashes'

Rosemary McGinness has been Group HR Director of William Grant & Sons, a family-owned spirits company, since 2005. William Grant was established in 1887 and owns such brands as Glenfiddich malt whisky and Hendrick's gin. Since October 2011 she has also been Chair of Young Enterprise Scotland.

Rosemary told me of a great example of creativity when you have a crisis. The problem arose in 2010 when the Glenfiddich distillery roof collapsed under heavy snow. This could have been a disaster with a huge loss of revenue for Grants as the whisky became exposed to the elements. However, as staff worked to clear the snow and rescue hundreds of barrels exposed to the cold, it occurred to distiller Brian Kinsman that the malt within the barrels could be saved as a fantastic non-aged single malt.

Malt master Brian Kinsman mentioned at the time that a photographer was shooting and, rather fittingly, when he looked at the pictures, the light shining through the roof looked like a phoenix rising. So that day 'Snow Phoenix' was born. Snow Phoenix is described on the Grants website 'as a single malt of stunning complexity, balance and elegance. Rich apple pie flavours entwine with aromatic honey, finishing with a smoky, mocha back note'.

Sue O'Brien, CEO of Norman Broadbent, recounted a story of when they were merging two businesses and had two loyal receptionists from both organizations. The board could not decide between them and were at a complete impasse. Instead of going down the traditional route of getting both of them to interview for the job, Sue suggested they write a business plan together about their role in greeting clients. They did, and called themselves 'front of house managers' and designed their own rotas and shifts. They both work full time now and the feedback from clients is wonderful. I have experienced it and it is. So Sue's ability not to go for an 'either or solution' when she was up against it was impressive.

In Focus

Kevin Beatty 'Sprinting at work'

A&N Media has, in addition to leading UK newspaper titles such as the *Daily Mail*, the *Mail on Sunday* and *Metro*, a portfolio that includes over 200 websites covering news, property, recruitment, retail and travel. Among these are a number of well-known brands, including Jobsite, JobRapido, Wowcher, Mail Travel and the world's number one English language newspaper website, Mail Online. CEO Kevin Beatty has been an Executive Director at Daily Mail and General Trust plc since December 2004.

Kevin told me that he firmly believes that creativity is 'simply good business behaviour and frankly we don't have a business unless we are creative'. The newspaper industry is interesting because it is so 'church and state', as he puts it. That often means creative and marketing people are in contest with sales and management people. He thinks that while managers in his business have always been seen as the convergers, that doesn't mean convergers aren't creative. Kevin wants the global management team to be seen as just as creative as the journalists and marketeers. He has set up an innovation team and Lord Rothermere, his chairman, is supportive of this initiative and is equally passionate about creativity at work.

The company wants to get ideas from everyone and so has set up an 'Ideas factory'. Before Kevin started this quest for innovation, an idea had to have a three-year business plan with spreadsheets. Now Kevin has stolen the idea of 'sprinting' from technology companies that release new technology in 'sprints'. First the sprint for ideas, then the 'productizing' of them and only after that do they create the business plan. Needless to say this has speeded up the programme of innovation exponentially.

And finally, when all else fails, even lawyers can be creative. Stephanie Liston, Partner with Charles Russell, LLP sent champagne-coloured roses to the CEO of a business who didn't use her for a deal. She got the next one!

So let's now revisit two of the myths discussed in the introduction to the book: 'creatives' are eccentric personalities who are seen as different from the rest of us and creativity is really about the arts and has no place in everyday life and certainly not business.

'Creatives' are eccentric personalities who are seen as different from the rest of us

When talking to artists, opera directors and designers I discovered that their creativity muscles were more exercised than the average but of course that is their currency. They often knew that they were creative from their early years. For example, artist Kate Downie says she was 'creative before I knew I was creative' but felt that all children are. She thinks that she has a conceptual way of looking at the world that might be different from others and also has a desire for eternal enquiry. She was passionate about art from the age of four or five. She looked at her crayons and had an emotional reaction to colour. So she is different perhaps, but not weirdly eccentric.

Creativity is really about the arts and has no place in everyday life and certainly not business

With all the stories of doing things differently and new ideas for products or services, I think that creativity at work is alive and well, but was very surprised that 70 per cent of our sample did not view it as such. So the myth that creativity is all about the arts persists but is not really borne out by the stories I have heard.

Steps to creativity at work

⭐ Enjoy knowing your creative style.

⭐ Give the questionnaire to your team to discover how diverse or not you are.

⭐ Realize that having ideas at work and problem solving is creative.

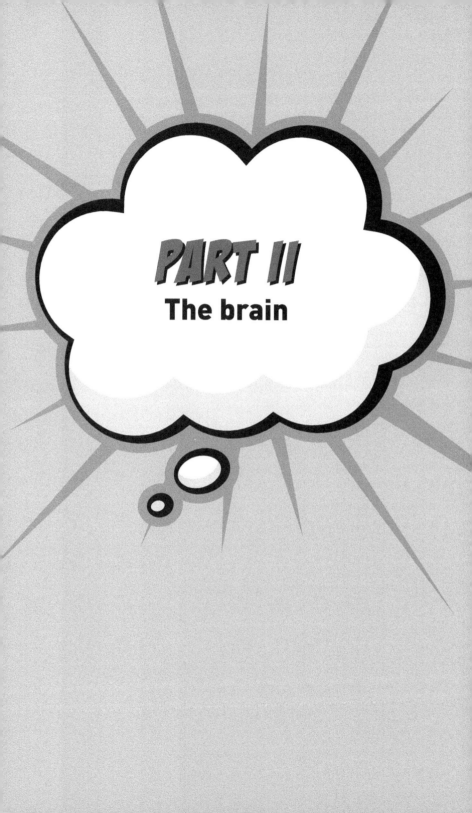

Thinking

I really needed to understand how creativity works. If we are all wired for creativity as the experts tell us, why are some people always coming up with wonderful life-changing ideas and others struggle to remember ever having had one? And there are other dichotomies that were exercising my brain. If we are rational creatures, where do feelings and 'aha' moments fit? Is creativity all about spontaneity, not dogged hard work? And where is right brain/left brain thinking in all of this? What a tangled web!

If creativity is an amalgam of thinking processes, should I not look at how we think and make everyday decisions before progressing to the rarer pastures of creative thinking? Let's start with a historical perspective about thinking and how it came to be that we believed ourselves to be rational creatures differentiated from the rest of the animal kingdom with its instincts and impulses.

Freud and icebergs

As a young psychologist I was brought up on Freud and the struggle of the Ego over the rampant and unruly Id, while negotiating with the conscience of the Superego. The essence of Freud's concept of the human psyche is that we are rational creatures once our Id has been supressed by our Ego. Let me explain further.

According to Freud, we are born with our Id. The Id is an important part of our personality because, as babies, it allows us to get our basic needs met. Freud believed that the Id is based on a pleasure principle. In other words, the Id wants whatever feels good at the time, with no consideration for the reality of the situation. When a child is hungry, the Id wants food, and therefore the child cries. When a baby is uncomfortable, in pain, too hot, too cold, or just wants attention, the Id makes its presence felt until a parent meets the need.

By age three the child interacts more with the world, and the second part of the personality begins to develop. Freud called this the Ego. The Ego is based on the 'reality' principle. It understands that other people have needs and desires and that sometimes being impulsive or selfish can hurt us in the long run. It's the Ego's job to meet the needs of the Id while taking into consideration the reality of the situation.

By the age of five, Freud states, that the Superego develops. The Superego develops due to the moral and ethical restraints placed on our behaviour. The Superego might be seen as our conscience as it dictates a belief in right and wrong.

According to Freud, the Ego is the strongest so that it can satisfy the needs of the Id, not upset the Superego, and still take into consideration the reality of all situations. In other words the Ego keeps a person rational. Conscious thought is but the tip of the iceberg, with preconscious and unconscious thought lurking beneath the surface; see Figure 6.1. So the concept that as human beings we are – or must become – rational creatures in control of our baser emotions was perpetuated by Freud but had its origins way before that with the Greek philosophers. Interestingly the repercussions of this thinking are still being felt today and have implications for creativity and creative thought at work.

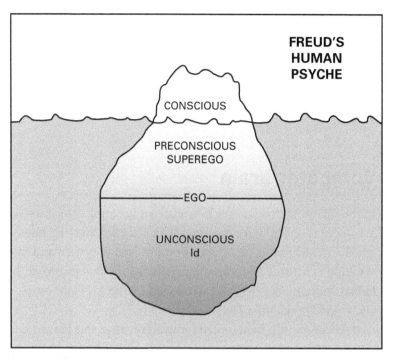

Figure 6.1 The iceberg model of Freud's concept of the human psyche

The Greek philosophers – Socrates and Plato

Greek philosophy is fundamentally about reason and the first amongst the acknowledged Greek philosophers was Socrates. Socrates never wrote on tablet, scroll or papyrus, so much of his work is gleaned through his student Plato, who was the author of a number of philosophical dialogues. These were essentially arguments that took the form of conversations; Socrates was a participant in many of these and thought to be Plato's mouth-piece. It was Plato's belief that abstractions or ideas, and not the material world revealed to us through the senses, possess the most fundamental kind of reality. This is not a million miles away from Freud with the rational Ego gaining an arm lock on the Id of the senses. It is no accident that 'platonic' relationships are known as ones devoid of passion and, according to Plato, on a higher plane than ones governed by lustful impulses. So for Plato thinking and decision making were totally rationally based.

Computer brain

In the 1960s, with advances in science and computer technology, a computational theory emerged which stated that the human mind and/or brain is an information processing system and that thinking is a form of computing. This theory was proposed by Hilary Putnam in 1961, and developed by the MIT philosopher and cognitive scientist Jerry Fodor.

It is commonly held as true nowadays that the brain takes input from the outside world to create outputs in the form of further mental or physical states. However, computational theory doesn't tackle emotional states such as pain or depression. Emotion is bundled up as 'qualia' and put to one side. So, no emotion permitted in this theory (unless met on television or in movies with depressed computers and upset androids!)

A theory that diverged from the concept of man as rational being, wrestling with base emotions, came at the turn of the 19th century from William James.

William James

William James, the American Psychologist, wrote in *The Principles of Psychology* in 1890 that homo sapiens is actually the most emotional creature of all. According to James we have as many if not more instincts, impulses and emotions than any other animal so we are not entirely the higher-order rational beings that for centuries we were presumed to be. James was the first such theorist to believe that these impulses and instincts were speedy ways of responding to our environment in comparison to more ponderous deliberate thinking. In terms of good decision making, James felt the skill was in knowing when to use each thinking style. He also had the idea that our thinking was a stream of consciousness not a succession of deliberate ideas. His observations paved the way for Aaron Beck and modern Cognitive Behaviour Therapy, which concentrates on our automatic thoughts and how they link to feelings and behaviour.

So here we have rational thoughts, automatic thoughts, impulses, instincts, emotions: what neuroscience underpins these ideas? What happens in our brains when we think or have an idea? And what does all of this have to do with creativity? Contrary to Plato, Freud and other advocates of the rationality of man, if we didn't have emotion, reason would go out the door. This discovery came after patients with frontal lobe brain damage were assessed. The outcome was that despite retaining all intellectual faculties these patients couldn't make a decision. They had become unemotional and were simply overwhelmed with detail as all options had the same weight. We make choices with feelings. So, contrary to Plato, who thought that pure reason was devoid of emotion, in fact nothing could be further from the truth ... and this was in the frontal cortex traditionally thought to be the home of higher-order rational thought.

There are four levels in the brain starting with the brain stem, which regulates the bodily functions of temperature, breathing and heartbeat; then the diencephalon, which is involved in hunger and sleep. The limbic system is the third level and the centre for emotions of violence, lust and impulsive, animalistic behaviour. The fourth upper level of the brain, the frontal cortex, is traditionally viewed as the source of intelligence and rationality. See Figure 6.2 for the placement of these four levels.

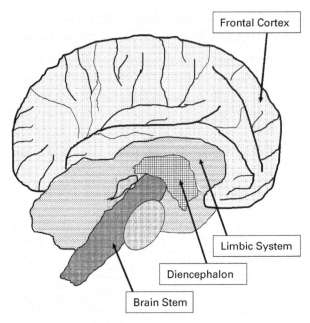

Figure 6.2 The four levels in the brain

Elevator brain

It was thought that the complexity of function rises as you go up the levels, from one to four. Figure 6.3 categorizes these functions from animalistic brainstem to the abstract thinking of the frontal cortex. However, the reality is even more complex with many links from the lower three levels to the frontal cortex.

Simply put, the top floor development of the frontal cortex placed us humans above any other animal as it emphasized our rationality. It was our differentiator, our evolutionary USP. And wrong!

The frontal cortex *is* involved with emotion, connecting the lower three levels with the upper-level thought processes. In particular it is the orbitofrontal cortex that integrates emotion into our decision-making process. And it is this link to our lower-order animal brain that allows us to make speedy decisions

- Abstract Thought
- Concrete Thought
- Affiliation
- Attachment
- Sexual Behaviour
- Emotional Reaction
- Movements
- Arousal
- Appetite
- Sleep
- Blood Pressure
- Heart Rate
- Body Temperature

Figure 6.3 Elevator brain – functions of the brain lower to higher

based on previous encounters and learning. So in fact we need both the upper *and* lower parts of our brain to make decisions, and the sub-basement has all sorts of back stairs to the top floors of our brains!

I wish I had been paid for the number of times I've worked with lawyers who tell me that they don't need coaching or training to become better leaders. Just give them the information and off they will go and do it. An hour, tops. In fact make it a breakfast briefing. But of course learning doesn't work that way. You need to connect emotionally to what changes have to be made. Being told is simply not enough to change behaviour. Even lawyers have an upper and lower brain.

Surprise, surprise!

Dopamine is a neurotransmitter that helps control the brain's reward and pleasure centres. It helps us decide amongst many options available to us, but it also triggers a 'surprise' response if something unexpected happens. Look at Figure 6.4 to see what a dopamine transmitter looks like (only very much smaller of course).

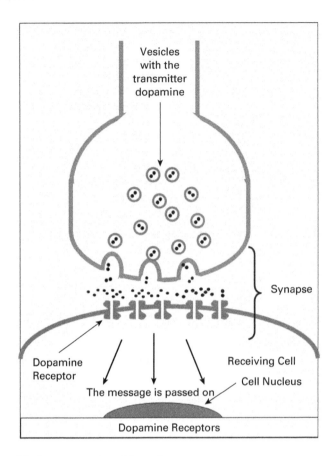

Figure 6.4 A representation of dopamine

There is a preponderance of these dopamine cells in an area of the brain called the anterior cingulate gyrus (ACC). This area of the brain, highlighted in Figure 6.5, acts as error monitor in addition to communicating with the limbic system comprising the thalamus, the attention getter, and the hypothalamus, which regulates bodily functions. It also helps us to remember mistakes. This in turn links with our autonomic nervous system that is associated with the fight and flight response.

So how does this work in practice? If you are asleep in bed and you hear a creak on the stairs you are suddenly propelled into

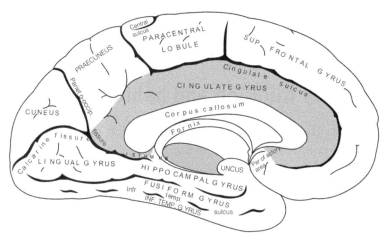

Figure 6.5 The anterior cingulate gyrus highlighted

wakefulness as you realize everyone was at home and in bed when you retired. You are then energized by your ACC, which has activated your autonomic nervous system to fight this potential assailant or run for your life. All of this happens in seconds. You only return to normality when you realize it is the cat or a thirsty child. And because the ACC is linked to learning and memory, when the creak is heard again you turn over and blame the cat.

Here's another example. I was walking along Princes Street in Edinburgh with one of my consultants. It was a balmy summer's day with no wind, which was unusual in itself for Edinburgh. Suddenly my companion fell to his knees, dragging me with him into a shop doorway. No, it wasn't my perfume or indeed a sudden proposal of marriage. My consultant had been in the army and when the 1 o'clock gun was fired as it does every day from the castle parapet, he was immediately transported back to the Falkland Islands where he had served. We received a few peculiar looks as we dusted ourselves down outside Russell and Bromley's shoe shop but afterwards discussed what an interesting example it was of dopamine triggering a knee-jerk reaction that had nothing to do with conscious thought.

So in summary, much of our thinking is emotional and not under our rational, conscious control. Plato – eat your heart out!

Speedy thinking and habits

William James was right when he wrote that our animal emotional brain was indeed a good thing as it led to speedy decisions that could be life-saving as many circumstances in which we find ourselves can't wait for slow frontal lobe consideration. Many women will testify that there was no logical reason why they felt uncomfortable when sitting next to a particular man in a bar. But those feelings might have helped save them from being mugged or worse.

As we learn we move from conscious consideration to automatic responses and habit. I remember when I learnt how to drive. With great deliberation I put my foot on the clutch, put the car in gear, released the handbrake, looked in the mirror, signalled and pulled out into road. I had to think carefully about each of these steps but of course I now drive like breathing – automatically. This saves us so much time and effort that it would be difficult to imagine a life lived entirely at the level of our frontal lobes.

Sometimes conscious thought can actually *interfere* with highly learnt responses. I am thinking about singers and actors who suddenly freeze on stage. It happens to the best. Sir Laurence Olivier famously suffered stage fright in 1964 and developed strange behaviour in order to concentrate on his lines. I have worked with air traffic controllers who had previously got a buzz out of bringing planes down as close to each other as possible (within the rules of course), but then suddenly questioned their skills after a minor incident, finding it difficult to return to work. And there are professional golfers who decided to rethink their swing, which they had at that stage in their careers taken for granted, and became paralysed by doubt in their ability. In all cases these people have 'over thought' what they have done naturally for years. Of course these problems can be helped by relaxation and cognitive therapy but they can become debilitating if not treated. Conscious thought can have a deleterious effect on our lives if not understood.

So what does all of this have to do with thinking, decision making and creativity at work? Well, thinking in the workplace is just as emotional, as habitual as elsewhere in our lives. To believe we are rational because we are at work is a foolish assumption and a dangerous one. Many decisions are made in the name of rationality without any thinking whatsoever!

Slower, more considered rational thinking is devoutly to be wished for on many occasions at work, so let's explore that. The knee jerk, the spontaneous, the instinctive is not always right.

Rational thinking

The prefrontal cortex (see Figure 6.6 for its position in the brain) has control over emotion and a jolly good thing too if we want to live in a functioning society. Constant unbridled emotion would be an exhausting thing. So our level four cortex acts as a filter and decision maker for which emotions it is deemed suitable to express, and of course these are dependent on circumstances.

I was coaching a director of an engineering company who had an exceedingly bad temper. Because he got over his outbursts quickly he had no idea that others did not. He was often heard to say after shouting at some poor minion, 'No hard feelings then.' Of course there were hard feelings; he was roundly hated. But he had a senior position so no one said anything. It took the CEO to organize some coaching sessions as anyone else would have been disregarded.

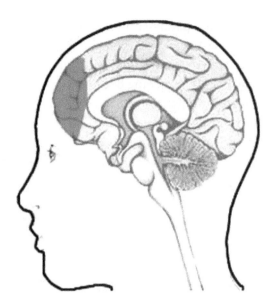

Figure 6.6 The prefrontal cortex

Some recent research into conflict at work reveals that not only is the performance of the recipient of the shouting diminished substantially but the performance of those overhearing the outburst is diminished too. In short, something had to be done. I explained to him about research carried out into the effect of anger on coronary heart disease and how by losing his temper he was putting his wellbeing at risk. We looked at the effect on his arteries of the stress effect of his anger and I also reinforced the concept that someone else's stupidity could be shortening his life. We contracted that he permit himself two occasions a year when he could lose his temper. That was a shock to him since he would shout more than that each day!

Two weeks after his first coaching session he had a meeting with the CEO and after an exchange of differences he paused and muttered ,'I've only got one left and this isn't worth it.' After a year we had a follow-up session and he told me with incredulity that he never did use his last permitted outburst as he came to realize that he could control his anger and influence others better without shouting. He was more relaxed, everyone around him was more relaxed and performance improved.

So rationality wins. And as much as emotion is a part of working life, unbridled emotion is damaging to all involved and requires the intervention of rational thought as a control.

Steps to creativity at work

✩ Reflect on how you think and make decisions. Are you always rational?

✩ How emotional are you at work and how could you control that emotion for more effective decision making?

Impediments to creative thinking

We discovered in the last chapter that we are more emotional and knee jerk in our thinking than certainly I ever thought, and we have retained that animal instant response that gets us out of trouble. However, there are downsides to that speedy thinking that can get in the way of creativity. I have investigated what these downsides are and there are many, so I have selected my top 10 favourites. Being aware of how we think helps us to navigate decision making and creative thinking with more confidence. See if you have personally experienced any of these glitches or have observed any at meetings you have attended.

Top 10 glitches

1	Just the data.	**6**	Low appetite for risk.
2	The optimist.	**7**	Polarized thinking.
3	The way we do things.	**8**	Stress.
4	Tricked by recency.	**9**	No review.
5	Group think.	**10**	No learning.

The top 10 glitches

1. Just the data

The figures are not looking good for the final quarter so an edict is sent from the board of the bank: reduce costs or 'lose head count'. A recently appointed head of department is horrified. He can't see a way to cut costs and as he has just hired his team it now looks as if he will have to lose most of them. With a heavy heart he writes an e-mail inviting his team to a briefing meeting.

Statistics arrive on the desk of the head of a regional National Health Service. It is a bill for translation services and it is huge. There were many African and Asian inhabitants in his area and if there were any illnesses and accidents involving this community, there had to be a translator present to enable a detailed history of events and symptoms. He immediately gets on the phone to get a reduced fee from the existing group of translators and at the same time e-mails HR to put the translation service out to tender.

Both of these stories reflect a situation familiar to all of us who have worked in organizations: immediate reaction demanded after the publication of statistics. No discussion, no thinking, just action to save money. Luckily there were advisers nearby who questioned these knee-jerk decisions and therefore the outcomes were very different. For the first scenario the head of department was encouraged to look at the problem differently and ended up adding 1p to the transaction costs and kept his staff. And for the second challenge, an Explorer in the team put forward the idea that they could help teach the communities English and focus particularly on the mothers who could then educate their children. This initiative had many positive consequences: the integration of local communities and an increased ability to verbalize their problems ... and a reduced translation bill.

The data is not enough for decisions to be made.

2. The optimist

Optimistic thinking is essential for success but it can cloud decision making. Optimism is only one thinking style we can adopt given the circumstances – and we all have the cognitive flaw whereby we look for evidence that confirms our beliefs rather than challenging them. So often I have seen people 'get' positive thinking, no matter what appalling circumstances they are in. They have the brainwashed look of the 'newly converted' and manage to squeak that everything is great despite all evidence to the contrary.

If things are really bad we have to be realistic. I remember seeing a set of figures delivered by our accountant. They were too good for what had been delivered, and as everyone else was celebrating the results I was accused of being negative as I puzzled over them. I asked for more information and on holiday a week later I heard from the accountant that his stats programme had a glitch and instead of delivering a profit we were running at a loss. In these circumstances is optimism appropriate? No – reality thinking is called for. All data was collected, options reviewed, scenarios proposed and voted on and actions taken. Of course circumstances improved and all were optimistic for the future. Optimism is not wishful thinking.

We should be a realist when making a decision and an optimist when implementing it.

Russo and Schoemaker

3. The way we do things

It's terribly tempting to think our ways are best and others are less rigorous. It stops us having to learn anything new.

When an employee of Microsoft joined the board of a very much smaller IT company, he was amused at how strongly they insisted that he went on their induction programme so that he learnt their ways of doing things. Not once did they ask how things were done in Microsoft. He saw so many ways that they could have changed their systems to be more efficient and profitable but he never put these forward. At board meetings he became aware that whenever he mentioned Microsoft there was a rolling of eyes heavenward. As he said, the time for him to see that small organization with 'new eyes' and be helpful was during the first six months. After that he would be truly inducted and one of 'them'. Sadly they were not humble enough to listen to his advice.

4. Tricked by recency

We tend to remember the first and the last things we hear – the primacy and recency effect. This is what I tell groups to improve their presentation skills so that they will start with a bang and end with more of a wow than a whimper. When your last memory is a year ago you tend to go with the recency effect. Sales people tend to remember the latest product when selling to clients, not the one that might be best for that individual. When leaders are carrying out annual performance management sessions with their direct reports both parties tend to remember the previous month's performance and not the sweep of a year.

I was renting out my apartment in London and latterly had the lodgers from hell. Broken crockery, water damage, constant complaints and all came with an amazingly aggressive attitude. I really wanted to keep this apartment but when I was made a reasonable offer for it I jumped at the chance. If I had done the arithmetic I would have hesitated but I completely forgot all of the other perfectly charming renters and only remembered the last difficult ones. Of course the apartment is now worth a fortune. You win some you lose some, but poor decision making on my part.

So when decisions are to be made, we tend to remember recent information and issues. Not always to good effect.

5. Group think

Surely if you put enough intelligent people in a room you will get a sound, rational result? No and not necessarily in that order. Conformity to an autocratic leader – no matter how intelligent a group can be – will deliver a biased outcome. Everyone agrees then mutters disagreement in the bar afterwards.

You probably know the Asch experiment of yesteryear. I even participated in setting one up at university. You show three lines to a group who are primed in advance to agree with each other, with the exception of one poor person who is ignorant of the set up. They are shown three lines that are clearly different in size and asked to declare if they are the same. All of the group agree in turn and more often than not the stooge agrees, clearly going against his or her perceptions to make that decision. We don't like to stand out or be in conflict so it is easier to be compliant.

Lack of diversity in teams especially boards can lead to questionable group thinking. I remember coaching a board director of a very successful computer company who was constantly in conflict with the rest of the board. He claimed that the top team was comprised of middle-aged men who had gone to the same school or type of school, lived in the same village with their children attending the same school. He was the lone voice of conflict as he came from a very different, working class background with an alternative perspective. They were very comfortable with each other, attending the same football matches at the weekend, which made for an easy life. My client didn't like football so yet again he was seen as the outsider. Of course that role can be so useful in that you avoid 'group think' but this group didn't see his contrariness that way. He had mentioned on many occasions that the company was ripe for a hostile takeover, but they ignored him. The company is not around today.

Where are the women?

Continuing the diversity theme, it would seem obvious that having more women on boards and a greater ethnic mix would help decision making from many different perspectives, but the influencer of 'similarity' gets in the way. I have described this effect in *Confidence at Work* and it is the comfort of the same that works against available facts. Cranfield School of Management has published some recent research and found that companies with more women on their boards outperformed rivals, with a 42 per cent higher return in sales, 66 per cent higher return on capital and 53 per cent higher return on equity.

In support of this diversity effect I remember running a series of team-building sessions for a large global company. The raison d'être was empowerment and decision making. We used an exercise that I haven't used for years. It was about being stuck in the desert after an aeroplane incident. You are provided with a number of helpful 'things' like a compass, a map, a mirror and other miscellany. What do you do? Stay where you are or venture into the desert? And what use do you make of the available tools?

We must have viewed at least a hundred of these teams wrestling with their decision making. The answer is to stay put. Experts say that you will not last long in the desert so better to stay where you are and use the map to put over your heads for shade rather than for planning your escape. The all-male groups metamorphosed into 'raiders of the lost ark' and 'gung-ho' desert crossers using map and compass as only intrepid desert crossers could. And of course they would be dead.

The best groups were a mixture of men and women or all women. Why? The mixed groups only worked when the women were assertive enough to counteract the male hunter-gatherer perspective. Comments from the women varied from, 'Well you will be going without me; I don't do deserts' to, 'Not me in my shoes' and they would put forward cogent arguments for staying put using the mirror as an alarm system to alert passing aircraft. This is apparently the thing to do so, for all readers who are caught in a desert, this is essential information!

The all-women groups worked well simply because they listened to each other. They allowed dissent and voted democratically at the end of debate: a skill that was markedly absent in the all-male groups, which tended to jostle for ascendancy. Each group of women voted to stay put and would have survived.

So, diversity challenges group think and aids good decision making.

6. Low appetite for risk

One of the simple rules in psychology is that working with either humans or animals you tend to get what you reward. Barbara Woodhouse all those years ago on television revealed how to train dogs, and more recently recalcitrant children were dealt with by 'The Nanny'.

In education it is now well known that you reward children for working hard, not for being clever. If you do the latter, when the children fail at something they feel stupid and are disinclined to try again or attempt more complex tasks. Stanford psychologist Carol Dweck, in her book *Mindset*, highlights the importance of choosing what you reward.

Grown-ups at work are not so different. If you reward 'right first time behaviour' then you might get fewer mistakes but you will also get fewer attempts at trying new things. Human behaviour is geared towards achieving reward and diminishing punishment, so if organizations want to get new ideas from everyone, they can neither blame nor punish when things go wrong with experiments. You simply don't get any more.

So to increase the workplace appetite for risk, failures must be tolerated. It was Howard Schultz of Starbucks who talked of fast failure being the way to institute new ideas. Keeping a close eye on outcomes and a preparedness to pull the idea if it is not working is, according to Schultz the way to progress (see more on this in Chapter 14). It seems that decisions can be geared to avoid risk if the corporate culture punishes and blames mistakes.

The Dweck experiment in 12 New York schools

There was an interesting experiment carried out in New York schools that highlights the power and language of feedback. For the study, researchers divided 128 fifth grade students into groups and gave them a simple IQ test. One group was told it did really well and must be very smart. The other group was told it did really well and must have worked hard. One group was praised for intelligence, the other for effort.

Asked if they wanted to take a slightly harder test, the kids praised for their intelligence were reluctant. Of those praised for their effort, however, 90 per cent were eager for a more challenging task. And on a final test the 'effort' group performed significantly better than the group praised for its intelligence. They also learnt from mistakes whereas the 'smart' group wanted to continue looking smart so didn't want to risk making mistakes.

---

7. Polarized thinking

Another thinking glitch beloved of individuals, organizations and indeed countries is polarized thinking. It tends to appear when something major has happened that generates extreme feelings.

Polarized thinking is alive and well in relationships. Think back to your teenage years when your heart was broken by the love of your life. That's it, you say. I am never going to go out again with … please tick box: a blonde, a brunette, an arts student, anyone good looking – whatever type you believed your lover to be. You might even have foresworn relations completely, for a while. So engulfed by emotion are we that we swing in entirely opposite directions in a bid to protect ourselves from future failure.

The equivalent in companies can be seen in the recent banking crisis. Mortgages were sold to people who ultimately couldn't afford them when the homeowners' jobs were lost. But in addition these mortgages were cleverly packaged and sold to investors. Bundles, which comprised a mixture of 'shaky' mortgages with 'dead certs', were traded. I remember being offered this investment and asking how it worked. 'What happens if folk can't pay these mortgages?' I asked. No one gave me reasonable answers.

When it was discovered that the banks were struggling with bad debt, their decision making became polarized; they made the terms of access to any form of lending so stringent that no one could afford to borrow. They swung from massive risk to complete security. The answer probably lay somewhere in between.

Countries swing politically, given challenging times. For example, given an economic downturn incumbent governments often experience voter swings against them even if that downturn is worldwide and they may have carried out sterling work attracting business to their shores. Barry Johnson, author and creator of 'polarity management', suggests that when there are complex problems to be managed rather than solved, polarity management works.

Return to work/stay at home polarity map

A recent client wanted to discuss the pros and cons of returning to work after maternity leave. Figure 7.1 shows the matrix we produced to help her decision making.

In reviewing the grid I asked my client how she could be in both plus quadrants to overcome her polarized either/or thinking. According to recent research her fears about her career being side-lined after maternity leave are realistic, so how can

Pluses for work	Pluses for home
Continue with career as a senior manager	More time with baby
Get to the top	Relaxed
Feel fulfilled	Time to do domestic chores
Intellectual stimulation	Time with partner
Break from domesticity	Time to learn to cook well
	Exploration of other work

Minuses for work	Minuses for home
Less time with baby	Bored
Stress of juggling home/work	Loss of position in company
Challenge of finding a nanny	No promotion
Exhaustion	Fear of domestication
No time for domestic chores	Less fulfilled
Less time with partner	More time with partner!

Figure 7.1 Matrix to help decision making

she continue her career but at the same time be around for her baby? With a list of questions generated by the polarities matrix we brainstormed her next steps.

Johnson emphasizes that the poles of a debate are always neutral and always have pluses and minuses attached. He describes a session he was facilitating with religious leaders who were strongly anti-apartheid. He was challenged to find a way of describing apartheid in neutral terms with positives and negatives. He came up with the concept of ethnicity. The joy of managing such polarities, even as polarizing and emotional as apartheid, is that you begin to see the positives from the other side's point of view which hugely helps negotiation and respect for differing opinion.

When problems have to be managed rather than solved, or the situation is complex and either/or thinking inappropriate, then examining polarized thinking helps to lay out alternatives clearly so that meaningful questions can be asked. For me the revelation and challenge is that you can work towards the positives in your polar opposites, which Barry Johnson calls both/and thinking, and stop relying only on either/or thinking.

8. Stress

It is our autonomic nervous system that is involved in the 'stress' response which, as we know from Chapter 6, is part of our lower animal brain. It dates back well before the development of our cerebral cortex, the home of cognitive processes such as decision making. Human brains still have the primitive responses for survival 'hard-wired' into the mechanism of response to stress and threats. These are still useful for survival so, when stressed, the more basic and primitive parts of the human brain take over.

Now, the kind of stress we were exposed to in prehistoric times was the sort that involved large animals intent on eating us, so we fought this threat or ran away. We now know the middle and lower brain can react more quickly to threats by preparing us to fight or flee. The logical, 'thinking' part of the upper brain shuts down and good decisions are placed lower as a survival priority. In our more complex society, with stressors ranging from over-work or job loss, to conflict at home, non-thinking reactions to stress can get us into trouble; decision making is impaired when we are stressed.

Stress and decision making

When we are stressed we can have several reactions that reduce effective decision making:

- *Our concentration is impaired.* There is too much internal distraction from our fear and stress. We become much more sensitive to environmental distractions.

- *There is a deterioration in our judgement and logical thinking* as our upper brain shuts down and we become more reactive, more knee jerk in our thinking.

- *We fear new ideas or activities* as a response to being overwhelmed and stressed. We tend to do things the way we have always done them, rather than using new ways or new technologies.

- *Our self-esteem and self-confidence can be undermined* as we are not thinking clearly and feel under threat. Negative thinking and self-criticism are not useful when trying to move forward in a positive direction.

- *We have less objectivity for the big picture* as we react to the minutiae of our fears. So there is no reality check that can show the overall position.

- *Creativity is reduced.* We see fewer alternatives and this reduces the brainstorming necessary for appropriate problem solving.

- *We tend not to data gather,* preferring to make quick, impulsive short-term decisions and failing to predict any long-term consequences. This can lead to serious mistakes.

- *We don't communicate well* with those around us and may be short-tempered due to all the stress hormones released into our bodies. So we fail to get input, to make good decisions and fail to motivate people to help with effective decision making.

9. No review

I think it goes without saying that it is the power of feedback, of review, that helps progress. So why for the most part do we not do it? Stress, work overload or perhaps a reluctance to look failure in the eye; or what might be nearer the truth is that we embellish the past and put a positive spin on our errors. There are many ways of doing this. We distort our memory, deny all knowledge or blame others for our mistakes.

All of the above happened with the Hillsborough disaster of 1989 in the UK where 96 football fans died in the Sheffield stadium. The documents about the disaster, released to the public in 2012, revealed the cover up by the police where statements were erased and the public blamed for the disaster. Somebody somewhere could not face up to the responsibility. And of course if there is cover up there is no proper review and so mistakes are repeated.

How we review is also important. Keeping some kind of log of decisions or thinking is key. I have noticed in therapy and then in coaching that once somebody has changed their thinking, feelings and behaviour, this is internalized and it is difficult for them to remember being any different. This assimilation is encouraged as it is important that they feel they have made the changes themselves. That is the power of good coaching. But when it comes to reviewing the therapy/coaching the changes experienced are often downplayed. Getting an accurate review should be carried out continuously, not just at the end of the programme. The fine detail of thinking and change has been forgotten as it has been adopted. For progress to happen continuously without the input of a professional, clients have to learn the self-awareness that results from reviewing their own thoughts, feelings and behaviour.

10. No learning

'Experience is inevitable; learning is not.' No review, no learning. At work we log performance, sales figures, profit and loss but all too rarely our thinking and decision making.

One board of my acquaintance had been on a review course and they had all decided that at the end of their board meetings they would take five minutes to review their decision making. At the very next meeting, which had taken all day – never a good idea – the chairman forgot about the review and it fell to the one female board member to remind them (just as they were packing up to go) what they had all contracted to do. With much huffing and puffing they spent a cursory few minutes remarking on how well they had done but with no reflections on learning. So paying lip-service to a review produces limited learning. Leading horses to water … comes to mind.

It is really difficult to change our thinking. The old lower brain habits die hard, which is why there are still conflicts in the world with the genesis of the hatred going back generations. William James puts it succinctly: 'A great many people think they are thinking when they are merely rearranging their prejudices.'

So, those were my top 10 glitches in thinking and decision making and all are impediments to creative thinking.

Steps to creativity at work

✪ Be aware of any glitches in your thinking as well as the thinking of those around you.

✪ Review the results of your own decision making.

✪ Are there any patterns? What did you learn?

The creative thought

We now understand how the brain works in terms of rational and emotional thinking and the impediments to creative thinking. Let's focus on what happens when we have a creative thought.

Think of a word that works equally well with the following words: *pine – crab – juice*. When I did this before embarking on this chapter I wrote out all three words and I could not get the word 'nut' out of my mind and this clouded my judgement. So I made myself a cup of coffee and bingo, there it was: apple.

This in a nutshell is what happens in the creative process or at least part of it – the 'aha' part. You are stumped to find a solution and then when you are not thinking about it an idea comes as if out of nowhere. And what is fascinating is that you literally do have a lightbulb moment. A part of your brain – the anterior superior temporal gyrus – has a burst of activity just before the idea comes to you. Look at Figure 8.1 to see the position on the surface of the right hemisphere just above your right ear.

Researchers Beeman and Kounios gave 18 people more than 120 puzzles in which they had to find a common word that linked three different words, like the puzzle above. They then monitored people solving puzzles with a MRI scan (magnetic resonance imaging) and an EEG (an electroencephalogram) and this part of the brain was shown to light up about 30 seconds

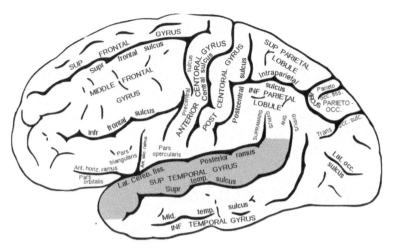

Figure 8.1 Anterior superior temporal gyrus

before they saw the solution. When using left brain analysis, no lights!

And do you know, it doesn't matter if you get the answer yourself or someone else tells you – your brain still lights up. Insight is insight. Here's another. Create 'new door' into one word. See the answer in italic, overleaf, if you are stumped. Your brain will still light up above your ear, I promise.

A colleague and I had a stumped moment the other day. We had to put some materials together rather quickly which described the company's offerings for a conference with HR directors. Previously I had some cards printed that described the details of Confidence at Work as a Confidence Cocktail with a picture of a flaming cocktail. It was a previous 'aha' I had at my publishers when I was trying to find a symbol that described confidence, and the cards had been a great hit. So I had suggested to my colleague over the phone that we do the same for each of our other products and find a symbol for each. He was against the idea as to him it was not a unified enough approach. The discussion got pretty heated till suddenly he went through a tunnel and lost phone signal. When he emerged he had the concept firmly in place. With the strap line, 'You don't need to gamble with us' he suggested we have playing cards printed with our products on the back of the jack, queen, king and ace. It was a wonderful idea which delighted our audience who did of course remember our company and what we did.

So, if a tunnel can help in the creative process, I wanted to discover why ....

The power of alpha

Again, EEG results help in this quest. Just before an 'aha' moment the brain fires off alpha waves that are associated with relaxation. In a relaxed state we are much more likely to see associations as our attention is directed internally; in the process of more logical analysis we are focused outside ourselves into the world of external stimuli.

new door is 'one word' rearranged

So that is why a shower, a bath, or somewhere relaxing helps to produce solutions to problems. Certainly when I ask groups of people around the world where they have their best ideas, they very rarely say at work. Holidays are a favourite time, or driving home after work.

Table 8.1 shows that when we are wide awake we are in Delta, with brain waves between 14 and 21 cycles per second. When we are in Alpha our brain waves reduce to between 7 and 14 cycles per second but we are not asleep. Most of us experience relaxation and Alpha in the hypnogogic or hypnopompic state – before we fall asleep or when we wake up in the morning. The trick is of course capturing the ideas that come to us before falling asleep or rushing out the door. This is why meditation can be so helpful to the creative process, apart from all of the other health benefits it can bring.

Table 8.1 Brain waves

	Cycles/sec	
Beta	14 – 21	Awake
Alpha	7 – 14	Light sleep/meditation
Theta	4 – 7	Sleep
Delta	0.5 – 4	Deep sleep

Archimedes had his Eureka moment when he was having a bath – probably a relaxing moment for him. According to legend, when Archimedes got into his bath and saw it overflow, he suddenly realized he could use water displacement to work out the volume and density of the King's crown without harming it.

Daydreams work pretty well too but you must be aware of them and have the ability to stop and capture the ideas they produce. The concept that when you are at work you must be constantly busy with no time for reflection is counter-productive. I hear so many stories of companies cutting breaks and embracing a 'long hours' policy regardless of European directives to the contrary. Time to think is for 'wimps' in these organizations.

Breakthrough thinking is just one type of creativity. There are many others, for example telling stories is creative and important in the learning process. One of the most fascinating insights from the split-brain studies I reviewed as a student was the way the left hemisphere made up stories to explain what the right hemisphere was up to. And since language is the provenance of the left brain, we can assume that creativity is not sourced purely in the right brain. So another myth dies – creativity is not just a right hemisphere activity. And this makes sense in relation to our exploration of different types of creativity in Part I of this book, with the blue sky, eureka thinking of the Explorer being just one of four styles – but a very essential one.

I do think many companies find Explorers too wacky for their streamlined operations. But every team needs at least one to produce 'ahas' and different outcomes. Part IV of the book looks at how you can increase the chances of having these cingulate gyrus moments and creatively supercharge your workplace.

Steps to creativity at work

☆ Reflect on when and where you have your best ideas and use that information so that you can produce new ideas when necessary.

☆ Give yourself time to think. Put it in your diary if it is not happening regularly.

☆ Learn the skill of relaxation. If you are stressed your 'aha' moments will be few and far between.

☆ Use stories to communicate creatively.

☆ Make sure you have at least one Explorer in your team.

PART III
Results

The creativity
at work survey

Part III delivers the results of a poll I conducted of 1,000 people at work in the UK. I then go on to explore why certain sectors are more creative than others and also how other nations might be faring creatively at work.

Having explored the brain and how we think, I came to realize that despite having an innate ability to be creative – which was present when we were children – this ability can be eroded by education and, dare I say it, by where we work. Discovering the glitches that stop us coming up with good rational decisions, never mind new ideas, revealed to me that creativity at work is not something easily achieved. In fact circumstances can be stacked against us ever being creative at all; add to that the discovery we explored in Part I that 70 per cent of our sample felt that creativity was the preserve of the arts and not the workplace.

I was beginning to understand why only 28 per cent of my face-to-face sample used any kind of technique to get ideas, and only 3 per cent used a process for creative problem solving. But I still didn't know if these opinions were widespread or just a particular view of this sample. So I conducted a poll of 1,000 people at work in the UK. I wanted results from those in current employment and in companies that were small to medium-sized enterprises; no start-ups or global players.

In terms of position in the company I asked for people to record whether they were a 'senior director, a managerial position or professional' or a junior position listed as 'supervisory, junior managerial, assistant'. The group were asked to choose from the following job sectors; we also asked about age, gender and the region of the UK in which they worked:

Agriculture

Arts and leisure

Catering and accommodation

Education

Health and social care services

IT and telecommunications

Manufacturing

Media and creative services

Mining, engineering and utilities

Personal services like hairdressing

Professional, business and finance

Retail, hire and repair

Wholesale

Do complete the survey yourself (see Figure 9.1) and compare your results with the poll sample of 1,000.

Rate each statement as it relates to your organization from 0 (do not agree – it does not happen in my organization) to 4 (strongly agree – it happens all the time in my organization)

Never happens: **0**	Rarely happens: **1**	Occasionally happens:**2**	Sometimes happens: **3**	Happens all the time:**4**

How do the statements below relate to the company you work for?

Talent

1. People are encouraged to develop their creative skills

2. Efforts are made to recruit people who think creatively

3. The most creative people are actively sought out by all managers

Energy

4. People are given time to think up new ideas

Method

5. Everyone systematically uses a creative tool or technique

Individual

6. Individuals are thanked all the time for their efforts

Team

7. Teams are trained in creativity and problem solving methods

Target

8. Creativity is at the top of my organization's agenda

System

9. Ideas are formally collected and processed

Ideas

10. New ideas are implemented all the time

Freedom

11. People are not afraid to challenge existing ways of doing things

Engagement

12. People's happiness at work is regularly surveyed and monitored

Humour

13. Most people agree that it's fun to work here

Risk

14. The failure of new ideas is seen as OK and no-one is blamed

Figure 9.1 Creativity at work survey

Add your scores for each question in the table below

Talent (total of first 3 scores)
Energy
Method
Resources – total score:

Individual
Team
Target
System
Process – total score:

Ideas
Freedom
Engagement
Humour
Risk
Culture – total score:

Total of 3 scores: **Average of 3 scores:**

Figure 9.1 *continued*

Composition and scores

Table 9.1 Profile of the sample

	%	Responses
Age range		
18–24	19.20	192
25–34	38.30	383
35–44	22.30	223
45–54	12.60	126
55+	7.60	76

Table 9.1 *continued*

	%	Responses
Gender		
Female	52.50	525
Male	47.50	475
Which of the following best describes your job position at work?		
Senior (Director, higher/intermediate managerial, professional, etc)	28.50	285
Junior (Supervisory, junior managerial, assistant, etc)	71.50	715
Region		
East Anglia	5.40	54
East Midlands	4.20	42
London	17.70	177
North East	4.40	44
North West	13.00	130
Northern Ireland	1.50	15
Scotland	7.80	78
South East	10.80	108
South West	8.70	87
Wales	5.40	54
West Midlands	10.90	109
Yorkshire and the Humber	10.20	102

Table 9.1 shows the breakdown of the sample by age, gender, job position and region. Table 9.2 includes the overall average scores for the total sample. The scores are out of a potential of four, so the range of scores shown, which are between one and two, means that creativity rarely or only occasionally happens on all of these questions. Figure 9.2 shows the mean scores for the total sample on all questions.

Table 9.2 Overall average scores for the total sample

Overall mean scores	
Talent	1.87
Energy	1.72
Method	1.61
Resources	**1.73**
Individual	1.91
Team	1.68
Target	1.42
System	1.85
Process	**1.72**
Ideas	1.91
Freedom	2.01
Engagement	1.86
Humour	1.62
Risk	1.83
Culture	**1.85**

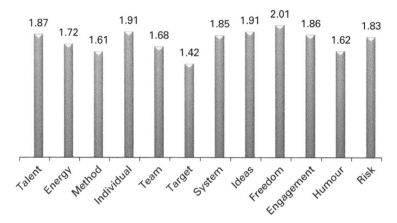

Figure 9.2 Mean scores for the total sample on all questions

Figure 9.2 perhaps reveals more clearly where the peaks and troughs lie in the overall results. The lowest mean score of 1.42 was achieved on the question: 'Creativity is at the top of my organization's agenda.' Next at 1.61 was: 'Everyone systematically uses a creative tool or technique', closely followed at 1.62 by: 'Most people agree that it's fun to work here.' The highest mean score achieved was 2.01 on 'People are not afraid to challenge existing ways of doing things' but it still only represented a rating of 'occasionally'.

Let's look at the percentages of the total sample in Table 9.3 and how they scored on each question. The highest score is achieved on question 11, with 36 per cent of the sample agreeing with 'people are not afraid to challenge existing ways of doing things' followed by Question 1 with 35 per cent rating 'people are encouraged to develop their creative skills' as happening in their workplace, and question 6 at 34 per cent with 'individuals are thanked all the time for their efforts'. Of course this means that 64 per cent of the sample and more are not scoring positively on any of these questions about creativity in their workplace. Lowest again with only 22 per cent is question 8: 'creativity

Table 9.3 Percentage of the total sample scoring on each question

How does this statement relate to the company you work for?	Overall sample of 1,000 people at work in the UK (%)
1 People are encouraged to develop their creative skills.	35
2 Efforts are made to recruit people who think creatively.	31
3 The most creative people are actively sought out by all managers.	29
4 People are given time to think up new ideas.	25
5 Everyone systematically uses a creative tool or technique.	25
6 Individuals are thanked all the time for their efforts.	34
7 Teams are trained in creativity and problem-solving methods.	26
8 Creativity is at the top of my organization's agenda.	22
9 Ideas are formally collected and processed.	32
10 New ideas are implemented all the time.	30
11 People are not afraid to challenge existing ways of doing things.	36
12 People's happiness at work is regularly surveyed and monitored.	33
13 Most people agree that it's fun to work here.	25
14 The failure of new ideas is seen as OK with no one blamed.	29

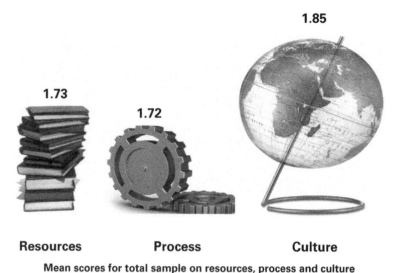

1.85

1.73

1.72

| Resources | Process | Culture |

Mean scores for total sample on resources, process and culture

Figure 9.3 A pictorial representation of the results

is at the top of my organization's agenda' – so creativity is not at the top of 78 per cent of our samples' company agendas.

Figure 9.3 is a pictorial representation of the results. 'Resources' covers questions on talent, energy and having a creative method to come up with ideas. 'Process' comprises individual, team, target and system, covering praising input, training teams in creativity, having creativity at the top of the company agenda and having a formal process for collecting ideas. 'Culture' involves questions on the implementation of new ideas, challenging existing ways, as well as happiness, fun and failure.

When the average means of the three summary scores of resources, process and culture are plotted, culture is the healthiest score of the three, but again still below two, so in the 'rarely' category. There were no significant differences in scores across the regions of the UK and there were no significant differences between the sexes with the exception of the question 'New ideas are implemented all the time' where the women in the sample scored higher than men.

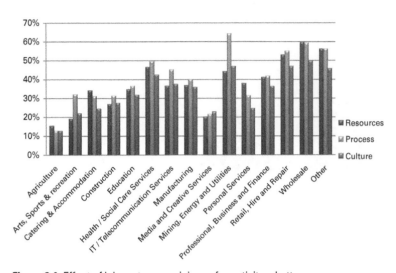

Figure 9.4 Effect of job sector on opinions of creativity – bottom scores

Figure 9.4 represents the different job sectors and the percentage of lowest scores achieved in the survey for the three overall areas of resources, process and culture. In other words, people surveyed scored zero or one meaning they rated questions about creativity as never happening or rarely happening at their workplace. Notable is the 64 per cent of people from the mining, energy and utilities sector who chose the lowest score for having a creative process at work. In other words, 64 per cent of these companies don't have a process at all or only occasionally. Wholesale, retail, hire and repair, and health and social care are not far behind in the low scoring stakes.

On a more positive note, 50 per cent of those in arts, sport and recreation sectors chose top scores of three and four on resource, process and culture as well as media and creative services, which averaged 45 per cent (see Figure 9.5). Construction achieved a 40 per cent score and catering 35 per cent but the highest scoring sector for creativity at work is agriculture. The other job sectors scored between 20 and 30 per cent, which is

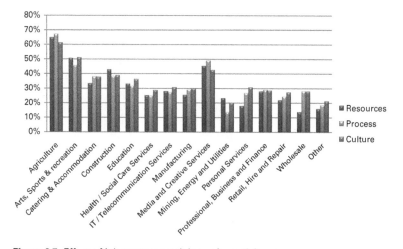

Figure 9.5 Effect of job sector on opinions of creativity – top scores

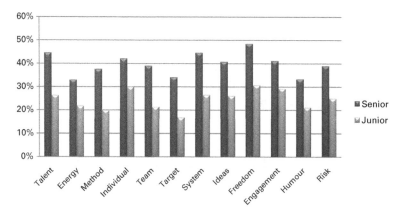

Figure 9.6 Effect of job position on opinions of creativity – top scores

poor as it means that between 70 and 80 per cent are rating their organizations badly in terms of creative resources, process and culture.

Another significant result was job position and the choice of top scores. Figure 9.6 shows that senior managers had significantly better opinions about their organization's creativity than

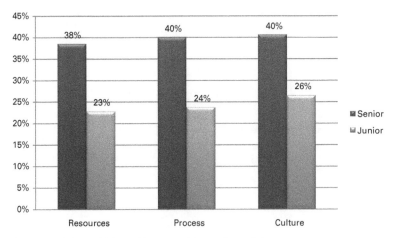

Figure 9.7 Effect of job position on opinions of creativity – resources, process and culture

junior managers. This score was significant on all 14 questions, as seen in the top graph. When the scores were amalgamated into the three factors of resources, process and culture you can see more clearly the significant difference in results across all three totals (Figure 9.7).

Summary of the results

- On average only 30 per cent of our sample felt that their companies in the UK are doing anything substantial about creativity.

- Agriculture, arts, leisure and media were the best job sectors in terms of creativity but were still achieving only 50 per cent on all three measures.

- The lowest scores were achieved on questions of companies having creativity at the top of their agenda, people consistently using a problem technique and it being fun to work there.

- There was a significant divide between senior positions and junior roles on all survey questions, with senior people having better opinions about their companies in terms of creativity than more junior employees. The implication here might be the lack of involvement of younger people in their companies' creative initiatives or perhaps they had higher expectations.

Sector spotlights

Let's explore the three sectors that scored the highest (though still not that high) on the poll, I think we can understand why arts and leisure and media – social or otherwise – might score highly. Those involved in these sectors earn their living by coming up with leading edge ideas, but agriculture? Let's have a look at why these three sectors score higher than the rest on all indices of creativity at work, and one low-scoring area, the public sector. Lest we think all public sector agencies are tarred with the same brush, I present Lambeth Council in London, later in this chapter.

Agriculture

CASE STUDY

Spotlight on: farming in Surrey, England

Jac Macdonald used to have a beef herd of 200 but now he has a dairy herd. He used to make a reasonable living but now he has to adapt or die. What happened?

The economy happened. The big supermarkets happened. Jac's from farming stock – fourth generation on a medium-sized farm in Surrey, England.

When I spoke to him he likened his situation to running from the trenches – people all around are falling but so far 'not me'. Part of the reason is that Jac is unusually adaptable. His family had reared beef for generations but university-educated Jac saw that the numbers simply no longer added up. He was losing about £100 a head on his beef after all costs had been taken into account. At this point a lot of farmers have simply persisted and run at a potentially ruinous deficit. Not Jac. He knew he had a good herd and against family opposition he sold it and got a very good price. Now at this point a lot of people would've turned the farm into a boarding house and sold the land to a builder, but he bought a dairy herd, to produce milk and of course other cows and bulls, which is more productive than selling animals for slaughter. With this new business model Jac's business is flourishing but only just breaking even. This is because some large supermarkets and manufacturers are reluctant to pay what the farmers consider the fair market price. And the reason for that, Jac tells me, is – us. We've all stopped drinking whole milk. The cost of cream has plummeted by about £800 a tonne in the last year, squeezing the manufacturers who then squeeze the farmers.

He and others are tangling on a daily basis with these realities and are even offering limited milk deliveries to local customers, which of course doesn't solve the global problem but means that Jac's vans are making daily contact with customers who are buying the new line of farm-house food that Jac has diversified into. His steak pies are a wonder, but so far you can only get them in Surrey until he opens his online shop later this year.

By being adaptable and realistic Jac has developed other income streams around his core investment.

Spotlight on: farming in Kanturk, Ireland

Liam Philpott now relies on heavy machinery rather than farm hands and has adapted well to the technological changes in his industry. He says it's more cost-effective. In addition, he feels a freedom to trial ideas and decide whether they work or not. For example when the newly born lambs were dying during a tough winter, Liam brought them into pens nearer the farmhouse, but they were still succumbing to the cold. His wife Anne had the ingenious notion of strapping them with baby monitors so they would know if the lambs were distressed and could then intervene speedily to save them. This is an excellent example of a small idea that produces big results, which is something that we can all relate to.

Spotlight on: farming in India

ITC is one of India's foremost private sector companies with a market capitalization of US$35 billion and a turnover of US$7 billion. It is rated among the world's best big companies.

ITC's Agri-Business is one of India's largest exporters of agricultural products. The ITC group's contribution to foreign exchange earnings over the last 10 years amounted to nearly US$4.9 billion, of which agriculture exports constituted 56 per cent. The company has helped Indian agriculture significantly by empowering Indian farmers through the use of the internet. This transformational strategy, which has already become the subject matter of a case study at Harvard Business School, is expected to create for ITC a huge rural distribution infrastructure.

Abhishek Jain is a soya famer in Raisen District India. Here he tells his story:

Before ITC, we were restricted to selling our produce in the local 'mandi'. We had to go through middlemen and prices were low. ITC trained me to manage the internet kiosk and I became the internet guy in my village. Today we are a community of e-farmers with access to daily prices of a variety of crops in India and abroad. This helps us to get the best price. We can also find out about many other important things – weather forecasts, the latest farming techniques, crop insurance. This has not only changed the quality of our lives, but our entire outlook.

So in England, Ireland and India, farmers are using technology to change the way they work.

Arts and leisure

You might expect the arts and leisure to be more focused on creativity as it is their lifeblood and, frankly, what they are paid to deliver.

CASE STUDY

Spotlight on: Charles Monteith Walker, Scottish artist

Charles Monteith Walker was born in 1957 in Falkirk and in the mid-1990s his style began to evolve after several visits to Italy, Spain and Portugal. The warmth of light and colour, the piazzas, churches and towns provided him with a new, rich source of inspiration and led to the development of his own distinctive, unique style.

His work has become increasingly bolder in colour and composition, mixing imagery, symbols and shapes from a variety of different sources both geographic and historical. Charles is versatile in what he paints, moving easily from landscapes and still life to imaginative, vibrantly coloured compositions using thick layers of oil paint that give his paintings a strong almost sculptural quality. He is now regarded as one of the most original contemporary Scottish artists.

Charles is my cousin so I know how he goes about his work. He is often driven to paint through the night to finish a composition, surviving on plentiful cups of coffee. I met him in London and I could see that all before him in the Chinese restaurant where we were eating was grist to his artistic mill. He watched the faces around us with an intensity of curiosity and discovery. It was the same outside in Leicester Square where he took photographs of the most mundane objects, which to him were captivating.

The creative learning we can take from artists like Charles is their desire for new perspectives and a willingness to travel to achieve this fresh look. Do we visit and travel to get fresh perspectives for our work and take that travel seriously as a creative tool?

Next is his curiosity. I was working with some unemployed young people and we were talking about curiosity. They told me that they always walked around looking at the ground, lost in their thoughts. They saw nothing. Understandably they were preoccupied with their jobless situation but I challenged them to look intently around them, noticing details that had previously passed them by so that they could come up with ideas for work.

Another example of such creativity was experienced during the opening ceremony of the Olympic Games.

CASE STUDY

Spotlight on: Olympic Games opening ceremony

The opening ceremony of the Olympic Games showcased a British take on both the arts and leisure. Danny Boyle's presentation of all that is British was captivating, humorous and compelling.

Live sheep, Victorian smokestacks, maids dancing around maypoles, a tribute to the National Health Service with 10,000 medical workers tending to sick children in large hospital beds, a Bond-like David Beckham in a speedboat racing down The Thames to deliver the torch to the stadium and of course the Queen with the proper James Bond. All from Danny Boyle's vision of true 'Britishness'. There was history, old pop stars and younger ones, pensioners and pearly kings and queens, Shakespeare and Minis. This was an inclusive pageant of all ages, races and creeds alive in Britain today.

And it was the clever use of LED lights that made the ceremony spectacular: that and the use of the huge central space with people and things flying overhead that lent a true air of excitement and circus. What the world made of it I am not sure but it was certainly a showcase for creativity at work in arts and leisure in the UK.

The learning I took from this ceremony was that everything is open to creativity, from the Queen to the NHS. Everything contributes to ideas at work and that surely includes the professions, which are often reluctant to embrace creativity.

Technology and social media

CASE STUDY

Spotlight on: Google, United States

Let's look at Google to see if there are transferable skills for us in our businesses.

Google, founded in 1998 by Sergei Brin and Larry Page as a result of a grad school project, is now a multi-billion dollar company. The Google search engine is like breathing – we just can't do without it. One secret of Google it seems to me is its constant desire for new products, which it tests with new users to obtain feedback. It keeps its creativity crackling. Every member of staff is encouraged to come up with completely new ideas and given time off each week to do just that. Apparently in the fields around head office people in anoraks are often to be seen staring at horizons or communing with nature. The ethos is that you problem solve first then the money will follow.

Brin and Page, despite being multi-millionaires, are still hands-on in the business and both focus on what they love. They are renowned for fast-paced change. Another secret to success was the arrival of Eric E Schmidt as Executive Chairman. Since joining Google in 2001, Schmidt has helped grow the company from a Silicon Valley start-up to a global leader in technology. As Executive Chairman, he is responsible for the external matters of Google: building partnerships and broader business relationships, as well as advising the CEO and senior leadership on business and policy issues. This left Sergei and Larry to do what they do best – focus on the technology and creativity of the company. They are now working, I believe, on downloading a map of the human genome so that we, the customer, can download our own DNA. Larry Page, commenting on his success, has said that optimism is really important for companies to move forward and 'You've got to be a bit silly about your goals.'

The creative learning from Google is the rampant desire for the new and that staff are actively encouraged to have and pursue new ideas. Where a culture of creativity is free to flourish, so can profit and reputation. It's true, perhaps creativity alone cannot guarantee global success, but as an advert for new talent and investment, what better reputation to have?

The other interesting point for leaders is the freeing of creative talent by having the business and commercial side handled by those who do that well and not the creative people, as that is simply not their strength.

CASE STUDY

Spotlight on: Unitedstyles, China

Unitedstyles, based in China, is an online youth fashion store accessed only through Facebook. It is a Facebook Connect-enabled service. Young people and their parents can choose and design their clothes in 3D; their creations are produced on demand and delivered anywhere in the world.

Unitedstyles has three founders: Dirk, Marc and Xander. They have different business backgrounds: marketing, internet and fashion and complementary skills. The founders are rebels who want to fundamentally challenge the fashion industry. Marc van der Chijs says that his objective is to recreate the entire fashion design experience for internet users: 'It's very strange that you cannot already design your own clothes online.'

They chose Shanghai for their head office as they feel that this city is bursting with energy and attracts young and ambitious people not only from all corners of China but also from the rest of the world. Their view is that:

Chinese people are industrious, innovative, and entrepreneurial and open minded. It's the best place in the world to start a company that merges IT with fashion and vice versa. There is both a large textile industry, nowadays including top class high-end production, and a huge IT sector (no country has more people online than China and the centre of IT is Shanghai).

The dominant business strategy in fashion is to guess months in advance what a customer will want, and Unitedstyles wants to reverse this. 'We change the fashion industry from a "push" into a customer "pull" model,'

Marc van der Chijs, who also founded the 'Chinese YouTube' Tudou, says. 'Because of mass production, clothes have become cheaper but also less personalized. Tailors hardly exist anymore, or are considered too expensive.'

With Unitedstyles users can replicate their own 'tailored' experience, choosing from a variety of styles, prints, colours and shapes (there are several charts to check sizing). They outsource all garment production to Chinese digital textile printers, and because it doesn't create any of its own inventory, it avoids the traditional fashion industry downside of surplus product.

The creative learning from this example is tapping into the youthful desire for individuality and style while accessing the technology that they use daily – Facebook. It is enabling the customers' creativity in an easily accessible way.

CASE STUDY

Spotlight on: redbus.in, India

In 2005 Phanindra Sama was frantically running around Bangalore hunting for a last-minute bus ticket to take him back home for the festival of Diwali. Despite calling travel agents and racing through the city's traffic, he failed to get a seat and had to return home. He wondered why there was no centralized booking system for bus tickets in India when 'plane and train bookings were so well catered for'.

His company, RedBus, spent years unifying the system – bus operators, tickets, travel agents – and now has **www.redbus.in** that serves more than 10,000 bus routes. Customers can view seats from multiple operators, purchase tickets, and post ratings about service. Meanwhile, bus operators can track seat availability, and travel agents can pre-book passengers. RedBus tripled sales last year, adding 4.25 million passengers.

The creative learning here is that there are countless examples of glitches in systems, poor customer care, or an absence in a market of what you would like to be available. That is a gap you can exploit for business gain. Fill that with your own targeted product or service, because if you require it others might too.

Public sector

CASE STUDY

Spotlight on Lambeth Council, UK

The public sector may not have achieved high scores on the creativity survey but Lambeth Council, London, is bucking the trend. It is striving to change the traditional council paternalism to offer a range of options to the public, all of which is driven by public sector cuts. After two years of discussions it accumulated 35 recommendations about how to revolutionize services. For example, it has launched a website cooperative called 'Made in Lambeth' which allows developers and designers to work together.

Some students from London Southbank University noticed that there was a lot of scrubby unkempt land surrounding GP surgeries so they have formed a cooperative and planted fruit and veg to be used by the local health trust. So they eat the produce then sell the surplus to local hospitals ... and the gardening helps the depressed and isolated. Many wins.

- They have launched 'Barbeque on a Bike' offering food and friendship to disaffected young people on street corners.
- They have a 'Love your Space' initiative where residents can post photographs of plots, land or derelict spaces deemed eyesores that they would like to reclaim.
- The staff from cemeteries and crematoriums had the great idea of Skyping relatives during funerals and also taking videos to send to absent friends.
- A Lambeth inhabitant, worried about children in her area who went to school on empty stomachs, started 'Magic Breakfasts' for school

children. Now 6,000 primary school kids are served a magic breakfast every morning.

Jo Cleary, Director of Social Services, tells me the secret of their success has been the permission to fail. Lambeth CEO Derrick Anderson has made it clear that each project is an experiment, a test bed of ideas, and that no one involved should fear failure.

All of these ideas and more were captured by an artist at their Leadership Network meeting and every department has now viewed this pictorial vision of Lambeth's future. Which is looking pretty good!

Spotlight on: the US government. Todd Park, US chief technology officer

Todd tells us that there's an extraordinary amount of innovation happening in the US government, and the single biggest driver is that the government is embracing the idea of open innovation – unleashing the power of the private, academic and not-for-profit sectors, and the public in general, to get a lot more done than if the government tried to do everything itself.

One story is the Health Data Initiative. There's a lot of data in the vaults of the US Government Human and Health Services; data on everything from the health of communities, the quality of health care providers and information about drugs. The first thing that was done was to make available, in a user-friendly form, data that's never been made available before, either to the public or to qualified entities, while protecting privacy.

Entrepreneurs and innovators were told that the data exists and is accessible. To do this, tactics were used that were relatively unconventional for the government: meet-ups and gatherings called 'Datapaloozas' that started in 2010.

The Datapaloozas were key. Forty leading minds in the technology and health care sectors were invited to a meeting and a pile of data was supplied. They were asked, 'If you had this data, what would you do with it?' Over the course of about eight hours, they brainstormed different applications and services. At the end of the meeting, they were challenged to come to the first Health Datapalooza, 90 days later, to see if they could actually build what they had just brainstormed. The two criteria for products and services at Datapaloozas are that they must provide concrete value and have a sustainable business model. Well, these innovators showed up 90 days later with more than 20 brand new or upgraded products and services.

The Datapalooza had two important effects. One, it inspired entrepreneurs and innovators to get involved; two, it provided ammunition to liberate more data. Some people within the government were adopting a 'wait and see' attitude about data liberation. They weren't ideologically opposed – just busy. They were invited to the Datapalooza, and when they saw that in 90 days these amazing innovators had taken open data and turned it into fully functional new products and services to advance their mission, they were blown away.

For both of these public sector examples, government – local or central – had the bravery to go 'public' to ask for ideas and suggestions and trusted that their creativity would produce results. There is an abundance of ideas waiting to happen, but:

- You have to ask people to be involved.
- You have to teach them the techniques of brainstorming to get the best results.
- You have to act on the results.
- You have to take the risk of some not working to achieve the success of the others.
- You can create your own Datapalooza. People will be inspired by the name alone!

Cross-cultural perspectives

Creativity at work in China

Interview with an Area Director for Greater China, and Board Director of four Asia Pacific boards

My interviewee (who cannot be named for political reasons) would argue that China is the home of creativity. For five centuries it was the mother of invention, from the creation of vast infrastructures to the foundation of banking.

Today, after a lull during the Cultural Revolution, China is gradually asserting itself as a creative powerhouse; this will take time as the focus has been to provide manufacturing output for the developed world using Chinese labour and resources. Such a model is unsustainable as labour costs rise, so attention is very much turning to innovation and creativity. The speed of this change is much criticized, mainly by those who feel creativity is drained by too much bureaucracy and process. He thinks this is overstated, but it is certainly true in the State-owned enterprises. Creativity was restricted between Mao and Deng for roughly 30 years, but things have changed – the thriving arts scene is part of that renaissance as is the growing number of Chinese billionaires who are willing to be seen to pay very high prices for everything they use.

One other reason for China to look to creativity and innovation is the desire to become a truly international player; China's strategy requires the ability to compete with the world. Some examples would be its lead in new industries such as solar energy, hybrid cars, IT hardware and superfast rail travel.

Creativity is applauded in China: innovation parks and centres have been the focus of government work in many provinces and cities in China including Shanghai and Guangzhou. However, progress is lagging behind in production and manufacturing expertise. China's blog and twitter scene is one of the biggest in the world and although periodically censored, they are the veins through which much discussion about trends in fashion, music, style and celebrity travel.

China will become even more creative as it competes on the world stage. If we look at Chinese fashion and design, the Shanghai and Hong Kong fashion weeks are becoming mainstays on the calendar. In the world of consumer goods there will be more and more creativity in packaging, product and pricing to demonstrate to non-Chinese consumers the true value of Chinese food, tea, tobacco and alcohol.

Gone are the days of a supply model economy. China is rapidly changing to a demand model where consumers want and will pay for differentiation. My interviewee also believes improvement in supply chains out of China will help develop the image of Chinese goods and thus encourage creativity.

The new leader of China said it quite well at his inaugural press conference when he spoke of improving the lives of everyone in China, and this cannot be done without creativity in every aspect of life. However, the underlying hypothesis that China lacks creativity and innovation holds a lot of water internationally and is widely commented on. The Chinese public sector is certainly lacking in creativity and requires a makeover.

Creativity at work in India

Devesh Kapur, Professor of Political Science and Director of the Centre for the Advanced Study of India, University of Pennsylvania

Devesh thinks that there are several forces shaping creativity and innovation in contemporary India. First, the sheer heterogeneity and diversity of Indian society makes it a fertile ground for ideas and creativity. A second powerful force is demographic: the combination of a huge population, half of which is under 25; the entry of newly empowered socially marginalized communities into the mainstream of Indian economic, social and political life; and dramatic changes in the aspirations of India's young, empowered by new media technologies.

The third driver is rapid change in technology. This is allowing even those Indians with modest resources to leapfrog technologies by leveraging free open-source software such as Skype, cloud computing and cloud-based office tools. The ubiquity of cell-phone ownership means that it has emerged as one of the most egalitarian technologies, sparking creative, low-cost solutions for a range of challenges India faces.

Last but not least is the Indian state. Regrettably, its poor performance puts greater pressure for ideas and innovations on issues that it should be addressing but is unwilling or unable to do. Where the state retains its monopolies – in defence, security, land allocation, urban utilities and mining – there is considerably less innovation unless new entities are created outside the traditional government apparatus.

Multinational corporations have established more than 600 captive R&D centres across India. These include not only centres for IT firms such as Google and Microsoft that are drawn to India's specialized knowledge, but also engineering firms. As companies such as General Electric and Philips, and increasingly pharmaceutical firms, move away from having one large R&D centre in their home country to a more distributed global model, India is emerging as a global innovation hub.

Creativity at work in the United States

David Horth, Director of the Centre of Creative Leadership in the United States

David says:

Creativity is definitely not generally embedded in everyday work practice. This surprised me a little when I first came to the United States. Some of the same things I had experienced and the stories I hear are similar about innovation being rare and driven by a small population of courageous and often politically savvy individuals. However there is a much more can-do attitude and still a rampant optimism.

He tells the story about interviewing people in his previous company ICL in the UK with the question, 'What do you do when someone comes to you with a new idea?' One senior marketing person said that if you lined 100 people against the wall and machine-gunned them down, unfortunately another

100 people with ideas would stand up and they would also have to be mowed down: 'Why can't people do what they're supposed to be doing?' For him strategy was king. Another more soft-hearted manager of a software team responded: 'I tell them to take the afternoon off!' He asked why. 'In the hope that the idea goes away!' Everyone he tells this to in the United States gets a laugh out of it and also recognizes that this is more or less the norm there too.

Some organizations, he says, have deliberately developed a culture of innovation: the Googles of the world, the Cirque du Soleils. He has been talking recently with a US government agency that is working on its innovation culture but it will, according to David, be a hard hill to climb. 'The way they are dealing with innovation is for the usual suspects in research and development to take on the mantle and Six Sigma (the process improvement set of tools and skills) is for the process oriented–operational parts of the organization.' He believes that the polarity of Six Sigma *and* innovation is a solvable polarity but has to be recognized as such with both poles being embraced and the organization recognizing the upside and the downside of both and thus becoming aware of when the dynamic balance is out of kilter.

In summary

There are bursts of glorious creativity around the world with the internet playing a central role. However, creativity is not happening consistently in businesses, so how can we be innovative as nations when the basic tools and techniques of creativity are not in place? Innovation demands the skills of creativity.

Steps to creativity at work

★ Complete the creativity at work survey.

★ Review the questions on which you achieved low scores and take action. Read the next two chapters to discover what to do to become more creative at work.

★ Learn from the giants of creativity like Google – take time to think creatively yourself and with your teams, be optimistic about your organizations and a bit silly with your goals!

PART IV
Supercharging your workplace

Discover adjacent possibles

Part III revealed that companies are not being consistently creative at work. So how can we improve things? Part IV explores different concepts and environments that are conducive to creativity and has some skills for creativity to suggest.

In this chapter I review the concept of the adjacent possible, which describes how the chances of having an 'aha' experience can be increased. Add to that the concept of 'Q' and how happiness and respect increase creativity at work and I defy you not to feel more creative by the end, or at least have the urge to be more creative.

Let's start with the concept of the adjacent possible as it describes much of the creative process individually and in groups. It is the personal 'aha' *and* the group brainstorm. It was coined by Stuart Kauffman, an American theoretical biologist who studies the origins of life on Earth. He came up with the concept of the 'adjacent possible' to describe the various reactions in our primordial soup that led to life on earth – there was a series of relentless changes and movements, with each innovation leading to many new possibilities. But this concept does not have to be limited to soup, primordial or otherwise. The adjacent possible describes other creative connections so well. The idea is that once there is progress in one sphere it leads to an influx of ideas and uses in another. Many of these discoveries are serendipitous, as indeed our origins in all probability were.

Some adjacent possibles

The Teflon story

It is a common belief that Teflon, like Velcro, is a spin-off product from NASA space projects. However, that's incorrect, even though both products have been used by NASA. Teflon was accidentally discovered in 1938 by Roy Plunkett, in New Jersey, while he was working for Kinetic Chemicals. As Plunkett was attempting to make a new refrigerant, the gas in its pressure bottle stopped flowing before the bottle's weight had dropped to the point showing it was empty. Since Plunkett was measuring the amount of gas used by weighing the bottle, he became curious as to the source of the weight, and finally resorted to sawing the bottle apart. Inside, he found it coated with a waxy white material that was oddly slippery. Kinetic Chemicals patented the new fluorinated plastic in 1941, and registered the Teflon trademark in 1945. Some diverse uses for Teflon include domestic appliances, gaseous exchange membranes, grafts in biomedical applications; and the manufacture of stopcocks, glass fibres, transformers, plumbing tape and computer mice; solid fuel rocket propellants, cells used in spectrometers, containers and magnetic stirrers.

... and the Teflon coat

In 1969, Bob Gore independently discovered expanded Teflon and introduced it to the public under the trademark Gore-Tex. Gore-Tex is a waterproof breathable fabric and the company has now diversified into shoes and gloves. Gore-Tex is still thriving and is one of the top five companies to work for today.

Carbon fibre strength

Carbon fibre is another example of the adjacent possible. The high tensile strength of carbon fibre was discovered in 1963 in a process developed by Watt, Phillips and Johnson at the Royal Aircraft Establishment at Farnborough, Hampshire, and the process was patented by the UK Ministry of Defence.

The properties of carbon fibres, such as stiffness, high tensile strength, low weight, high chemical resistance, high temperature tolerance and low thermal expansion make them very popular in aerospace, civil engineering and the military. They are stronger than steel and much lighter. Golfers in the pursuit of the perfect golf club – and aren't they always – started to use carbon fibre clubs and gained speed strength and accuracy. My colleague and my husband wax lyrical when describing their carbon fibre clubs. Not so sure about the golf, however.

It's all in the cards

Next time you go to the supermarket and before you 'insert your card into the chip and pin device' you are likely to be asked to swipe your loyalty card. You'll probably do it, because you've been taught to believe that pounds mean points. And to some extent they do – although in my experience, like Airmiles, you spend a lot of pounds to get not very many points. But let that pass. They encourage you to swipe, not because they really want to give you money; they encourage you to swipe because it gives *them* information – information about your spending patterns, information about general spending trends, information about stock levels – information, and lots of it. It's by no means a new idea. In the 18th century companies gave away redeemable copper tokens; by 1891 trading stamps were all the rage; cigarette cards followed shortly thereafter and, hard on their heels, coupons, cereal box prizes – anything to make people stick with a brand. Clearly, people like to feel that they're getting a bargain, but these 'give aways' didn't really give the merchants very much in the way of information, just more volume.

So what's this to do with creativity? Let's look at what happens when some highly creative individuals meet some disruptive technology, put two and two together, and hit the jackpot. For that we must drift over to the shady alleys and squares of Barcelona. There, in the shadow of the cathedral of La Sagrada Familia, lies an unremarkable branch of a well-known Spanish supermarket. And yet here were set down the first roots of a great consumer revolution.

CASE STUDY

Spotlight on: Caprabo, the Spanish supermarket

They knew about barcode. It had been around since the 1950s and invented for the transport of cattle. They even used it to identify products and to speed up check out. But what, they asked, would happen if we linked the barcode to stock control? Well, that would mean more retail space. You wouldn't have to have on-premises inventory. And could we put the inventory in a centralized, climate-controlled robotic warehouse? And could we then trigger a message, based on dwindling stock levels, to instruct the warehouse to send us more inventory? Yes, they discovered they could.

'But wait a minute, this is all about us. What's in it for the customer? Could we somehow involve the customer in this food chain?' Behold the supermarket loyalty card. Not only does the technology help the supermarket, it rewards you for returning again and again. It helps the shop save money (by not sending you promotions that it knows from your purchase patterns are irrelevant to you) and what helps it save money, helps drive down the prices to complete what looks like a virtuous win-win circle.

Adjacent impossibles

Sadly people can have ideas which, from our more sophisticated perspective, are ahead of their time. This happens when the technology or means has not evolved or has not been discovered to put their ideas into action.

Historical examples

Jules Verne designed a rocket that would be destined never to enter space; unfortunately he was born before his time and the technology was simply not available to him. He was prescient but powerless. And of course we have Michelangelo, who mapped out a helicopter but again – no parallel technology, no viable product.

Current example

Some examples of the adjacent impossible are alive today. Here is one:

There was a problem with emissions and pollution from the stack of an ocean-going vessel – a big ship. Ships are our greatest polluters but not many people know that. John Young, a chemical engineer, came up with a very creative solution to inject hot air into the exhaust stack, thus dispersing the fumes. The challenge was to get the hot air evenly distributed 360° round the inside of the stack. He invented a circular 'bustle' which when pressurized from a fan gave the correct distribution and a cushion of air. This fan was up to two metres in diameter and was very successful at the job it was designed to do.

James Dyson, a British inventor, used the same concept for his new domestic fan. Sadly John, who invented the technology many years earlier, never made the connection to the domestic market and Dyson became the millionaire. John lacked the adjacent possible so it never occurred to him that it might work in a reduced form for domestic use. Dyson did. Hey ho.

Steps to creativity at work

☆ Be aware that seeing connections from another sphere and applying them to your work is at the heart of creativity. How could you see more connections? Do you need to get out more to experience other areas of business?

☆ Become interested in new technology, always asking yourself how you could use that in your business.

Creative environments

The big question for business is, or should be, what kind of environment and culture work best for creativity. If companies are to take creativity seriously then pursuing what enhances creativity would be sensible. This chapter delivers guidance.

Q

A concept called 'Q' was proposed by Brian Uzzi, a sociologist at Northwestern. He undertook an epic study of Broadway musicals, analysing the collaborations behind them and what differentiated successful and unsuccessful shows – flops. He was particularly interested in what made the perfect team deliver a successful show, musical or play. He coined the concept of Q, whereby the amount of Q denoted degrees of closeness and social intimacy of the people working together on a show. The question was, should the ideal team be composed of those who know each other really well and have worked together before, or do completely new faces bring a breath of fresh air to the creative mix?

Uzzi found that when people didn't know each other, had few connections and never worked with each other before (as

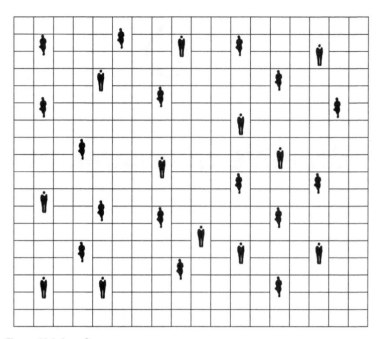

Figure 11.1 Low Q

represented in Figure 11.1), then their creative endeavours were more likely to end in failure. They simply found it too difficult to collaborate and exchange ideas.

If you can extrapolate Q to the general workplace (and it really wasn't designed for that but the concept is worth pursuing in this context), do we expect people to work together globally who haven't met each other and have no relationships except by conference call or, if lucky, once a year at an away day? Is this scattering of a workforce destined for failure or are there ways of involving people to ensure contributions and ideas are noticed and tracked?

Having worked with many global companies, I have put together some guidelines for keeping in touch using web technology.

Global team tips

If starting a new team or hiring a new team member, begin where possible with a face-to-face meeting. The 'getting to know you' is accelerated. If using psychometrics (which every good leader should use whether they are global or not), carry out the debrief face-to-face. So much can be misunderstood if tests are not fully explained and those on the receiving end can think the results immutable, which they are not. They are a great short cut to understanding strengths, and a huge help in working out how to target individual motivation and communication. Sharing CVs, photographs and perhaps, if everyone agrees, their psychometric test results, helps to create relationships.

If communicating via video, telephone or internet conferencing, it's important that this happens more regularly than office-based meetings. You can bump into people when under the same roof but if the only bumping is by task-focused e-mail, your team will feel starved of support.

So many leaders I talk to find it a challenge to make their global team interactions fun. They are all too aware that team members could be playing Sudoku, washing the dishes or perhaps even working for someone else while they are 'present' at a teleconference. The leader ends up doing all the talking in a frenzied stand-up comedian way, trying to be inspirational online. Providing an agenda and getting the team to complete work in advance and present their findings in a succinct way are all things that can help to make these virtual meetings more compelling.

How you capture ideas and build on them from a distance is a challenge and I have discovered a great online Post-It device at en.linoit.com. There is a 'lino' board online which provides different Post-It colours and everyone can post ideas on the team board during the meeting. Try it out.

Evaluate constantly. An online anonymous questionnaire allows a snapshot of how a team are feeling about their support. You can also monitor the number of ideas received and problems solved by the team – and of course take immediate action if they are unhappy.

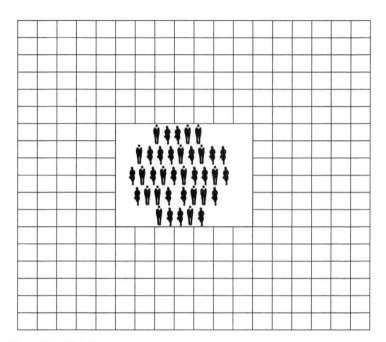

Figure 11.2 High Q

When Q is too high (everyone knows each other and have worked together before), when everyone is too comfortable with each other, they tend to think in similar ways – group think (see Figure 11.2). This also leads in Uzzi's terms to theatrical failure. Again we can extrapolate to the boardrooms of the nation: similar backgrounds, similar views, doing what they have always done, and little creativity.

So the ideal Q, as represented in Figure 11.3, shows a mixture of relationships; some close and others less so, or even new and fresh ones added to the group, the latter represented in the diagram by being further afield.

It is a challenge for large organizations to be creative. Initiatives start and then tail off, interested leaders come and go but the main issue is that the compliance of employees demanded by organizations works against ideas ever being heard, captured and acted upon. Large pharmaceutical organizations understand

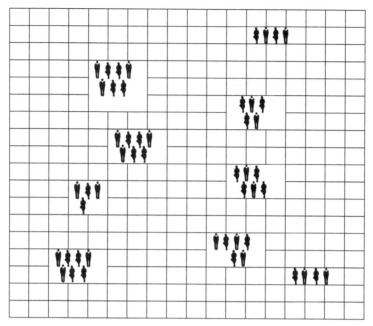

Figure 11.3 Ideal Q

this lack of creativity and buy smaller biotech companies to acquire their compounds for drug pipelines, which of course are their life-blood. The problem is that when these biotechs are absorbed they cease to be creative as they in turn become compliant to structures and processes.

In Focus

Interview with Steve Projan:
Technology meets pharmacology

Steve Projan is Vice President of Research and Development at Astra Zeneca Medimmune, United States. In 2012 he won Pharma Executive of the year for his role as lead during the transition of his team into infectious disease innovative medicine. I have worked with Steve and his team over the last eight years.

Maintaining small groups within smaller company structures seems to work better, as evidenced by an interview I had with Steve for this book. He tells me that the way the adjacent possible happens in science is in an ideal Q structure. Scientists at Astra Zeneca pursue new technologies as well as employing existing technology in new ways for antibody development. Steve claims that possible solutions, when scientists in different disciplines come together, are limitless. They are constantly discovering how something works from each other in different areas of research and then using that insight gained to try new things. As he says 'chance favours the prepared mind' – a favourite quote of his by Louis Pasteur.

He mentions that groups of scientists work in the same building so it is easy to get together. The size of their section of the company (around 4,000 people) means that people are constantly running into each other in hallways and canteens. According to Steve, it is this physical proximity yet separate groupings that makes a difference and leads to many incidences of the adjacent possible.

They are working right now on the 'half-life' of their drugs. Half-life is the time a drug takes to leave the body. Currently molecules of an anti-inflammatory have a half-life of two weeks but there is newly validated technology available and it can now be specifically focused on anti-arthritis drugs so injections are only necessary every three months instead of two weeks. If you are a sufferer, that must be bliss. Technology meets pharmacology in the hallways of science, creating the adjacent possible.

So how do you create the ideal Q in your team? Who might you invite into your meetings to give you that small but disparate group feel that mitigates the 'group think' discussed in Chapter 7? And what work environments fan the flames of creativity?

The outsider

What makes the ideal Q is the mixture of relationships along with the essential ingredient of the role of the outsider who brings a fresh perspective and new eyes. When I worked at Mobil before it joined forces with Exxon, it would regularly invite outsiders from different parts of the company to join in exploratory meetings. It found it was often the naïve question that moved people on.

In another example, young people can also be essential to the creativity process. As we discovered in our survey of 1,000 people in the UK, there is a significant divide between senior and junior managers. The former reported more creative involvement than their younger colleagues, and yet it is the fresh perspective that would enable more creativity at work.

Youth

Joeri Van den Berg, author of *How Cool Brands Stay Hot*, (Kogan Page, 2011) provides some startling insights into the thinking and buying behaviour of Generation Y (otherwise known as the Millennial Generation). According to him, their role models are their friends and parents. There is, in fact, little rebellion with this generation as they are used to empowerment and freedom from their parents, who have generally adopted a more coaching style to parenting. The traditional command and control authoritarian leadership we still have in British business today will certainly not go down well with Generation Y. They are simply more sophisticated than that. They also require constant stimulation; witness the wild success of the shop 'Forever 21', which changes its fashion offerings every day – every day, not every week!

They enjoy involvement and co-creation as that is what they are used to, for example in education and television. They like the authentic and the real. Openness is important to them and mistakes are OK if admitted. Happiness is important to them too and they are more emotional than previous generations.

Given they have buying power, why wouldn't you involve these young people in any debate about the future? They are 'oven ready' for creativity. Some of them are already digital millionaires at 18.

Women

Rationally it makes sense to have female representation on boards and senior management of companies given that women comprise 50 per cent of the populace. But we know that much thinking is not rational. Look at some of the most recent global statistics by Catalyst August 2012. Women's historical share of Fortune 500 board leadership in North America in 2011 was 8.3 per cent compared to 8.8 per cent in 2010. So we are going backwards not forwards. Women of colour on Fortune 500 boards in the United States in 2011 held 3.0 per cent of overall board seats, compared to 13.1 per cent of board seats held by white women.

Take a look at the graph in Figure 11.4 to view the position globally of board seats held by women. Europe's listed companies will be forced to reserve at least 40 per cent of their non-executive director board seats for women by 2020 or face fines and other sanctions under a proposal being drafted by the European Commission. The legislation is aimed at what EU officials believe is a severe gender imbalance across the bloc's 27 member states. EU data shows that in January 2012, women represented only 13.7 per cent of board positions in large listed companies. Although several EU countries – including France, Italy, Spain and the Netherlands – have already adopted their own national quotas, such hard limits have run into fierce resistance in Britain and Sweden, which currently have no restrictions.

The British Home Secretary and Business Secretary jointly commissioned Lord Davies in August 2010 to develop a strategy to increase the number of women on the boards of UK companies without resorting to quotas. For many women this process is just too slow. There are many subtle reasons why there is still a reluctance for women to be hired for senior positions. Men may have to change the way they do business, with more transparency and an increased focus on the interpersonal. They may also have to deal with challenge and conflict if these senior women are doing their job properly by providing an alternative view. Why would a board be bothered with this change when most don't in any way understand what behaviours women find unacceptable?

I had just completed a course with a major oil company about why women on the fast track had left the organization and set up their own companies or joined the competition. Research had revealed that as soon as the women got married the men started to ignore them, predicting that they would leave to have children. They certainly left but only because the men ignored them. Anyway, that isn't the story I want to tell. We were in the CEO's office after the course and he was asking for a debrief – he hadn't attended the course. I recounted how supportive and insightful a member of the board had been. The CEO said, 'Oh forget him, he's just a big girl's blouse!' He had absolutely no idea why we just stared at him. Money down the drain for that training then!

Women of course have to step up and put themselves forward for promoted posts, which in the past they have been all too reluctant to do. Their ability just to get on with the job and their expectation that fair play will prevail means that many senior women of merit are ignored.

Dealing with difference is not easy and I am not sure a board will willingly opt for that self-awareness and profound change. I have mentioned in my book *Confidence at Work* that the power of similarity is alive and well at senior levels despite statistics about the bottom line advantages of diversity. Research sponsored by Mazars in 2012 arrived at the same conclusion, so

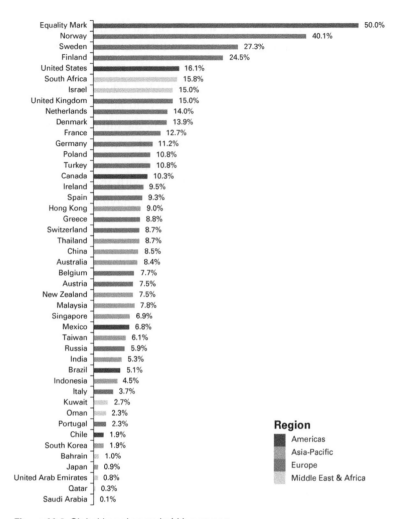

Figure 11.4 Global board seats held by women

it is with reluctance that I think that quotas may be the only way to motivate the entrenched senior males in the UK and around the world. Witness the success of quotas in Norway; the graph in Figure 11.4 shows it has the highest percentage – 40.1 – of women on boards.

If creativity at work is to be fostered, the more diversity achieved at board level, the better. But how can we achieve the fresh eyes of the outsider or the ingénue when we are slightly stale and jaded workers? Travel helps!

Travel

Anecdotal evidence has long held that creativity in artists and writers is associated with living in foreign parts. Rudyard Kipling, Pablo Picasso, Ernest Hemingway, Paul Gauguin, Samuel Beckett and others spent years dwelling abroad. Now a pair of psychologists, Maddux and Galinski, has proved that there is indeed a link.

They say that by adulthood, individuals have learnt how to 'dampen down' most areas of their brains in order to use one area to specifically focus on one thing. But babies and young children haven't yet developed the ability to pay attention intently on one thing, becoming captivated and enthralled by multiple stimuli, spreading their attention 'all over the place'.

When adults step into a foreign, unknown culture, the firing of neural networks occurs over the entire brain. The areas of the brain that adults have for so long dampened down again become saturated with neurochemicals, and processing takes place similar to that which occurs in a baby's brain. This type of thinking takes form as individuals realize that there are many different – and valid – ways of living in the world. There isn't one right way or viewpoint, and a single issue or problem often has multiple viewpoints or solutions.

Travelling abroad also presents multiple challenges, such as figuring out timetables for buses and trains, finding reasonable ways to shop and cook given a country's markets, and understanding cultural customs. Many of these challenges don't affect those who simply travel to other countries through planned tours, or are only in a foreign country for a short time.

There are some people and situations that just trigger creative thoughts and ideas. For example, I was visiting an outsourcing company in the City. All back office functions of banks and financial institutions were given to this company and when I was visiting its HR department I had a flood of business ideas. One in particular I seem to remember was about concierge services. The last time I visited the United States I was in Dallas and lost my way in a business tower block and ended up talking to the concierge. She ran her own business getting discounts for everyone in the building, from dry cleaning to free wine with dinner at local hostelries. My thinking was, why not creatively pinch this idea and franchise concierge services in London? I think those at the meeting felt I was mad and they couldn't have been less interested. But I became aware that travel does inspire creative thinking.

The benefits of taking a trip

- Three out of four executives believe that vacations prevent burnout (78 per cent) or that vacations improve their job performance (75 per cent).

- Two out of three executives believe that vacations improve their creativity (68 per cent).

- Travellers have a 25 per cent increase in performance on vigilance tests after returning from vacation. Travellers aged 45 or older show a 50 per cent increase in performance.

- More than half of employed Americans (53 per cent) state that they feel more connected with their families after returning from vacation.

- While on vacation, travellers rate their overall health one point higher (on a scale of one to five). They also get three times more deep sleep after their vacation and sleep almost 20 minutes longer after their vacation.

Cities

A theoretical physicist called Geoffrey West, along with a team of researchers, examined creativity in cities by means of counting patents, research and development establishments, inventors and creative professionals. What they discovered was fascinating. A city that was 10 times the size of a neighbouring one was not 10 times more creative – it was 17 times more creative. A metropolis 50 times bigger than a town was 130 times more creative. So as cities grow, ideas grow exponentially. It seems that despite the rough and tumble of a large city, with the overcrowding, noise and pollution, your average inhabitant is three times more creative than someone living in a town. More Q equals more adjacent possible!

In 2012 Richard Florida, the famous urban theorist, predicted that in 2050 cities will become bigger and life will become faster with the line between home and work becoming even more blurred. Richard states that cities will hold the key to a country's success as best practice will be carried out at a local level with initiatives in diversity and pollution control getting inhabitants engaged in creative dialogue. Mayors like Bloomberg and Boris Johnson will have even more power and they will be involved in driving change and innovation.

In Focus

The 'Glasgow Miracle'

Glasgow's Turner Prize winners

1996: Douglas Gordon

2005: Simon Starling

2009: Richard Wright

2010: Susan Philipsz

2011: Martin Boyce

▶

I saw Glasgow described recently on a BBC website by art curator Hans Ulrich Obrist as the 'Glasgow miracle'. I am intrigued by how Glasgow has managed to produce a generation of international contemporary artists, with an incredible number of nominations for Britain's top visual art award, the Turner prize.

The modern Glasgow art renaissance has its origins in the 1980s when a group of young artists including Douglas Gordon enrolled for a new course at Glasgow School of Art, led by David Harding. They had a new vision of art that was not about painting or sculpture or restricted to the studio. The course didn't take place in the Charles Rennie Mackintosh-designed Art School building that we all know and love but in a partially derelict former girls' high school around the corner. It was a place where the students could be a gang with total anarchy and freedom.

In the years after art school, Douglas Gordon founded the Transmission gallery in Glasgow. It was an artist-run space which they used as a laboratory and a showcase for the group's new ideas and energy. Simon Starling, who won the Turner prize in 2005, was a member of the Transmission committee and says that they all had a great sense of confidence. They could just get on the phone to their favourite artists anywhere in the world and invite them and they would come.

Transmission was a gallery that allowed the artists to take control. This concept really worked and, in the intervening years, the Glasgow School of Art has spread around the world and the now famous artists are still based in the city which moulded them initially. He says:

London is more difficult to work in. Glasgow is easier. People are more up for it and there is more space. People are less jaundiced and cynical, I find. I think it is important to be curious and have a child-like interest in the world. They are not in London so they don't think they have to satisfy the galleries. It's quite a good thing to have a distance from the art market because it means you don't get influenced by it and you just do your thing.

So a bit of adjacent possible, ideal Q and being an outsider really works for creativity.

Be happy

We all recognize creativity as poor starving artists in garrets or the depressed, troubled genius. And of course where anecdote exists then some truth lies. When creativity is internally focused, angst can be a driver. A young woman in my leadership class the other day was telling the group about the generations of famous artists in her family, but that this talent had bypassed her generation. The only time she feels an urge to draw is when she is very depressed. She had recently lost a baby and her feelings of grief produced an outpouring of artistic work that surprised her.

However, when you want to be focused externally, producing ideas for work yourself or in groups, happiness has the edge. A psychologist at Cornell University, Alice Isen, ran some experiments looking at the effect of emotion on creative problem solving. Participants were randomly assigned to groups, one to view a comedy film, the other a documentary about Nazi concentration camps. The happy 'comedy' group were significantly more likely to solve the creative problem.

In Focus

Professor Teresa Amabile: The power of happiness

Teresa Amabile, Harvard Professor, author of *The Progress Principle,* conducted some research in the course of which she asked over 200 workers from seven companies to keep a daily diary of events, feelings and actions over four months. The results were remarkable.

She discovered that despite not asking her research group about creative thinking they mentioned that they were much more creative on days when they were happy. Workplace happiness was mentioned in diaries when a leader provided positive feedback on progress. There was even a carryover effect lasting up to two days.

▶

A good mood has a lasting effect generating a greater variety of thinking and this led to new ideas at work.

Also, when new ideas were respected and rewarded by leaders – even if they turned out not to work – creativity increased. Support from their leaders was an essential component in their creative workplace performance. Where there was conflict and competition at the top, creativity was reduced.

Internal or 'intrinsic' motivation was a major factor too, with those who enjoyed the challenge of their work being more creative. Where there were promises of rewards, fear of poor evaluations, or competitiveness, the opposite was true. They were less creative. So 'worker of the month' schemes, she discovered, actually undermine creativity.

In another of her studies, 72 writers were randomly assigned to two groups and asked to complete a five-minute questionnaire: one group had questions about intrinsic motivation and the other about extrinsic motivation. The extrinsic questions were on literary success achieving financial rewards, and intrinsic ones were about the self-fulfilment of writing. There was a control group that read an unrelated story. All were then asked to write poetry immediately after their questionnaire experience, the creativity of which was assessed by external writers. The 'intrinsic' group were consistently and significantly assessed as being more creative. So, just five minutes contemplating financial rewards instead of intrinsic enjoyment had a negative impact on creativity.

So did the leaders in Teresa's study understand the power of providing feedback on progress or as she calls it, 'the power of small wins'? They did not. When asked what leadership skills made a difference to workforce performance they rated progress feedback at the bottom of the list. Small things really do make a big difference.

Respect your colleagues

Related to Teresa Amabile's research was a study carried out by Christine Porath and Amir Erez and reported in the *British*

Psychological Society Journal in July 2001. This study focused on rudeness. It was discovered that even if the recipient of rude behaviour did not embark on retribution or retaliation, performance plummets on measures of cognitive and creative tasks. Even those standing by and just witnessing the rudeness were affected.

But why is creativity impaired? Well, it was believed historically that creativity came unbidden from nowhere to the minds of the lucky. Now it is known that creativity requires concentration, the juggling of many ideas, and searching through loads of possibilities that then have to be integrated. Creativity demands agility and any interference disrupts cognitive resources and stifles the process.

In addition, those who witnessed the rudeness performed 20 per cent worse on an anagram test and produced 30 per cent less ideas when brainstorming than they did in a control group. Oswald and Parnes, the originators of brainstorming, always suggested that the suspension of judgement and criticism during brainstorming created more ideas, which as we can see is upheld here. Criticism of your ideas can so easily be felt as rude. So you shut up.

So how should you criticize without causing offence? A good working formula for providing feedback in most settings at work or at home is PPCO:

P: Pluses

P: Potential

C: Concerns

O: Overcoming concerns

The way PPCO works is that instead of jumping in to list your criticisms, justified or not, you need to control that impulse and look for some good in what is being offered. After this, be sure to talk about how you can see how that idea could be effective. Then and only then, you can air your concerns about the idea or solution. This can open up options for overcoming your concerns that you can proceed to discuss. I had a colleague who, calling on me from some far flung part of the world to hear what I had to say about some adjacent possible, would immediately exclaim: 'What a load of rubbish – it will never work' before I had finished a sentence. I ceased to share ideas as I was so discouraged. I decided, however, to share PPCO with him and I can now hear him hesitating as he searches for any worth in my ideas and it has led to a closer working relationship.

Steps to creativity at work

✡ Make sure your work environment is conducive to creativity – do you have a mix of people in teams to foster diversity?

✡ When travelling be curious about the country you are visiting. Leave the throng if you are on a package tour and explore on your own.

✡ How happy are your co-workers? Are small wins fed back to them as often as possible? If not receiving feedback from a boss ask for it, saying that you work better that way.

✡ Always show respect. Remember the fallout rudeness can create.

Creative skills for the workplace

So what have we learnt so far on our journey to understand creativity at work? Seventy per cent of my interview sample, despite citing creative ideas and innovation at work, thought creativity resided in the arts and that they themselves were not creative. This was reflected in my poll of 1,000 people at work that revealed between 70 and 80 per cent of companies are doing nothing or very little to foster creativity at work.

How can you encourage yourself, your teams and your organization to be empowered to come up with ideas, put your heads above the parapet and be more creative but keep the business going at the same time? These are the questions that define this chapter. Since we are all busy let's examine quick and easy ways that you can adopt to enhance creativity in your workplace.

How to enhance creativity in the workplace

Empower

Empowerment has become devalued as a concept as it is often seen as slick management-speak yet, call it what you will, it enables others to come up with ideas at work, and having the courage to voice them is an important skill for leaders of any variety. But how do you empower when you haven't ever empowered before? Here are two cautionary tales.

Bruce, a client of mine, volunteered to be in charge of employee engagement for the construction company where he was a director. He was a very people-focused man in an industry not renowned for it. A whole series of seminars was scheduled to include his team and their direct reports in planning the business strategy for the ensuing year. The first group of 40 were asked for ideas after an introduction from Bruce. Complete silence. Reconvening after a coffee break did nothing to loosen tongues. They tried again with more focus. There were some specific problems to be solved that required group input. Nothing came back from the audience; they just stared back in silence. What had gone wrong?

My question to him was how did he ever believe that his staff would suddenly be open with him and even speak up, never mind have ideas? So many organizations hire compliant candidates – and if they are mistakenly outspoken to begin with, they make sure that this is driven out early on. This company was no different. It had learnt to be an idea-free zone. A couple of round tables and a presentation were not enough to change the habits of a construction lifetime.

Another telecoms organization had a very sound idea of empowering its staff to call meetings on matters affecting them so they could problem solve on the job. This was started in the manufacturing division that made mobile phones, so the production lines were all involved. One day they were invited to a meeting with much razzmatazz and told that they were now empowered to make their own decisions. The very next day there was an issue with lunch breaks and the continuity of manning the machines. Some people did not want to wait for their break, so the lines were stopped and the whole plant had a meeting. By the time the meeting ended it was time to go home so no phones were produced that afternoon. After six months of meetings like this over a multiplicity of issues, the company went out of business and had to shut down. A truly wonderful idea wrongly executed. And you can just imagine a senior board saying, 'Well, we tried empowerment and look what happened. It just doesn't work.'

I would hate you to think that all such inclusive endeavours are prone to failure. So let me tell you about an example of success, again involving a telecoms manufacturing company, which wanted to develop self-managed teams on the shop floor, a little like those in the first example. To improve the production line they were given training in how to speak up and run good meetings, and a budget to bring consultants in for technical input. To this end, they ran their own team meetings without any management input. It was a huge success. Production output increased, the plant grew in size and employees were motivated and engaged.

Considering this looks so similar to the previous examples, what was the difference here? What should Bruce and the telecoms company have done to ensure an empowered workforce while not losing focus on the business? Here are some ideas:

- *Train* the workforce in communication skills and start gradually in small groups so that people aren't frightened to speak up. A group of 40 becomes a public speaking forum and scary. If it has to be a large group, break them up into teams of four or five.

- *Coach* all involved on how to run meetings with guidelines and good chairmanship skills.

- *Practise* the skills of problem solving by using the format that will be revealed in Part V of this book.

- *Educate* everyone about the profitability and targets of the business. It then becomes *their* business, and with that ownership comes intrinsic motivation of the kind Teresa Amabile talks about so compellingly.

- *Reward* individuals and teams for their ideas. These should not be large rewards or even financial ones. A personal thanks or a team mention is often enough. If an organization has rewarded compliance for years, allow some time for people to get used to new ways.

- *Promote* someone who is known to have ideas and word will spread at the speed of light. Come up with ideas and you will win approbation.

Without this, upfront input, empowerment will be destined for failure. But with some short focused skills input, empowerment can be transforming.

Be energetic

Ideas do not exist in a vacuum and they certainly do not happen in a meeting that is tedious and delivers only information. The challenge is, how can you make your meetings lively and energetic? The chap that turned around Avis Car Hire shortened and energized meetings by opening windows and taking all the chairs out so that people had to stand. He halved the time and generated drive. Perhaps drive to get out of a freezing room!

Having a creativity process helps too because group thinking tends to proceed along tram lines. Even the best endeavours produce similar results unless you can induce new ways of looking at issues. For that you need to get the team or group to use energizer techniques. Collect these and use different ones for each meeting. Become known as a team leader, director or MD who does things differently. For example, choose a different meeting room each week, ensure that people sit in a different seat each meeting, walk outside in summer, use art, music, sculpture to stimulate and energize. And of course supply feedback about progress.

New people are a rich source of fresh ideas as they have not been indoctrinated into the organization's ways of thinking.

Rich pickings to be had there, but instead of asking for their views, most companies have an induction programme that tells them how to change and be brought in line. None of your new thoughts round here mate!

Have courage

Doing things differently takes courage especially if no one around you has done anything new for years. Karen, one of my colleagues, mentioned that the company she is consulting for had major communication problems between managers and the shop floor. Put simply, they didn't speak. A new female executive arrived, and eschewed the corner office for a desk in the middle of the shop floor. This signalled a change as expectations were raised and dynamism returned.

I always like to try new things when training, so one day I had the courage to ask a group of bankers I worked with on a development programme to draw how they felt their week had gone. They looked at me as if I were mad but eventually succumbed and drew some stick figures. I would get them to present their masterpieces to the group and it always caused hilarity as their offerings would make their school art teachers weep. Of course proficient artistry was not the point of the exercise. It was to use different modalities for self-expression. I began to feel that this exercise was a little too 'out there' for the average banker and ceased to use it.

About two years later I had cause to meet a very senior manager in the bank who had been on my leadership course. He said that the major revelation for him was the drawing of his feelings at the start. It had been a release of pent up emotion about his job and that now he asked all his direct reports to produce drawings of how their month had gone at the beginning of their monthly meetings. It allowed him to tap into their predominant life events while at the same time encouraging self-expression. His meetings were so popular that his group used to arrive early to obtain the most commanding wall space for their art work. By now of course they were competitive, going to life drawing classes, watercolour groups, some painting in oils. And I had stopped using the technique while he had the courage to continue. Now I include it in our leadership programme.

It is worth asking individuals in your groups or teams when they discovered their voice – in other words, when they started to speak up about what they believed. The results are always fascinating. Of course this question, dear reader, is worth contemplating yourself. Many people mention their later years, perhaps at university or after they gained confidence at work. Some may still not have found their voice. Speaking up about how you think and feel is important for the creativity of your group so it is useful for a leader to know how voluble those around them are.

Be curious

To be creative you must be curious. If you walk around as if you are bored, looking at your feet, you will see nothing and therefore have nothing to contribute. Walk as if you are curious and you will always see things that give you ideas. Everything is interesting and ready for an adjacent possible connection.

Have a look at Figure 12.1 and think about how this wheelbarrow could be used. What were your first thoughts? They perhaps fall into two categories. *Option 1:* I can think of all the ways it can't work because it looks ridiculous. Wheelbarrows should have a wheel in the front not that silly prop at the back. It can't work. Never seen one like it! *Option 2:* It looks unusual but let's think how it might work. Perhaps if you have to work along a ledge, or where you can't tip something forward in a restricted space it could be useful.

Option 2 was the idea I had when I saw it. In fact this wheelbarrow is used on building sites as it can easily go round corners,

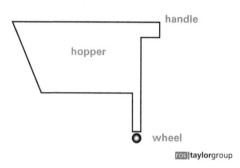

Figure 12.1 Design for a wheelbarrow

especially when on scaffolding. A normal wheelbarrow would get stuck.

It is very tempting to reject the unusual and say it can't work. Having a wild idea and taming it is a known way of coming up with something a bit different. There is a little saying, 'You can tame a lion but you can't make a pussycat roar.' In other words, it is difficult to breathe life into an old chestnut of an idea but you can certainly tame a beast of one.

To lead creativity you must search for the value in all new ideas. If you are dismissive then you won't get another. I remember Sir Ian McAllister, the CEO of Ford UK, telling me that he was given just such advice by a team of consultants. He had told one of his team that his idea was foolish during a meeting. He was taken aside afterwards and told that the toleration of the foolish was what his job was about.

Pay attention and notice things that others may not. My mother was always the one to notice the details of a car accident, robbery, even once a bank heist. She observed who was in which car, what they were wearing and even where they might have purchased their clothes. She was moving on to possible prices when the police signalled too much information.

One of my favourite exercises is the Potato Exercise created by Thiagi. Do look at his website www.thiagi.com as he creates a new business game every day and hundreds are freely available – so no excuses that you can't think of creative things to do with your teams. I met him last year for the first time and discovered that he is a man who is constantly creative, even over lunch.

Anyway, to the Potato Exercise. Each member of a group is given a potato. After they have examined their own potato in detail each person mixes it in with other potatoes at the same table. Potato owners are asked to recover their own potato. Most do. However, the potatoes are then added to an already existing heap of potatoes in the centre of the room and owners have to find their own potato. More difficult. Some people just grabbed any old potato, causing consternation in others who had bonded with theirs. On one occasion it was interesting to note that it was the director in charge of HR who chose his without any due diligence. A fight nearly broke out as another participant swept the room looking at each potato in turn for hers and found it in his grasp.

The feedback from this exercise was wonderful. Life was seen as analogous to being a potato or indeed a potato parent. You know your own. In the main what was mentioned was that participants had focused on something, an object, in a way that they had not done in a long time. Certainly not another person. We are all so rushed and deadline-driven that we have ceased to enjoy the detail of anything. Perhaps this is also a metaphor for leadership. No time to get to know those around you makes for a poor leader. *The Secret Life of the Potato* has to be my next book.

So be eternally curious and pay attention to what is going on around you. Life is more interesting that way. And getting into the detail can be profitable. Small things can produce big results.

Small ideas – big results

An hotelier friend of mine (he calls himself an inn-keeper) is one of the most creative people I know. He needs to be. He's in a cutthroat business. For instance, years ago, long before it was ubiquitous, he was offering free Wi-Fi in every room. His competitors thought he was crazy. *They* were milking their customers for an extra £10 a night. Guess who was right? Free Wi-Fi is now *de rigeur* (except sadly in France where I holidayed recently). I asked my friend if he thought this was his most creative commercial move. 'Oh no,' he replied airily. 'My best ever move was porridge.'

Margins were paper-thin. For example, for breakfast, they had to offer a choice, typically eggs, grapefruit, toast, porridge. The problem was people always ordered grapefruit. Why was that a problem? Because grapefruit had the lowest margin, followed by eggs followed by – you guessed it – the porridge. The question was "Who's *not* eating my porridge and more to the point – why not?' Well, the trouble with porridge is that, health benefits notwithstanding, it's a tad bland. So the chances of persuading a tourist to try it (more than once) are slim: unless, of course, you make it with milk and serve it with cream. That was the inn-keeper's creative masterstroke. Two extra words on a menu card: Porridge – with cream. That implicit hint of luxury (and no doubt the added taste) converted diners in their droves. Grapefruit? Bah!

On the one hand they sold a lot of porridge, but on the other they didn't use much cream at all. People regarded it as rather a luxury item to be used sparingly. Overall, and taking the cost of the cream into account, this simple move affected his margin by about 1 percentage point but increased his porridge sales by a factor of 10.

So what are some other small ideas that create big results? The one that my father never tired of telling me about was Swan Vesta matches. When first manufactured there was a strike pad down both sides of the box. An employee suggested that one side would be sufficient to strike matches and bingo, the company saved money and increased profits.

Another example was the young trainee who suggested they put one bolt in the production of a window blind instead of two and, bingo again, the company saved money and increased profits. And let's not forget the story of the leader of the bank team in Chapter 7 that charged an extra 1p on a transaction and as a result kept his newly formed team.

All of these small things lead to big outcomes. So often we think that creativity has to be about the big idea, the grandiose gesture. Not so.

Personalize things

A personal hobby or passion can contribute to and enhance creativity at work. Socializing with your work team helps you discover what they do in their spare time. Perhaps a 'bring your hobby to work' day would be enlightening. Who knows what you might get. If someone is a keen gardener, using gardening analogies when presenting his or her work would add spice and interest, or using growth as a model for work experience might be an interesting and personal take on the business. If you are interested in art, have art competitions or do as one IT consultant did and install an art gallery in the works canteen from the local art college.

Dentists are not renowned for their creativity (although perhaps I am maligning an entire profession erroneously). Certainly when I was looking for a new dentist I discovered a very leading-edge looking place near where I live in South East London. The decor was very 'nip/tuck' with much glass and stainless steel. But the most fascinating thing was the dentist himself. He looked a little like a pop star and I later discovered that was his true calling. As I arrived I was asked which music I would like to accompany my dental treatment. For a clean and polish I would usually go for some Stones classics; root canal was a more chilled Eric Clapton Unplugged and once for an extraction I chose some soothing Mozart. I discovered that you can hum with all that stuff in your mouth. Sadly, when the dentist left the practice to pursue his pop star career, the music stopped and the dentistry there was the poorer for it.

We shouldn't leave ourselves at home. There are many overlapping skills and all can help with making work more enjoyable.

Use imagination

Create a story, a metaphor, or a visual image to communicate something complex. I remember seeing an advert for a book in a Sunday supplement. It was about the brain and the latest thinking about how brains function. The journalist had likened this to a tree with different spurts of growth and this description caught my imagination. I rushed to the Amazon website. When the book arrived it was impenetrable. It was the journalist who had communicated well, sadly not the author.

Imagination is the precursor of creativity and as Ken Robinson says in his book *Out of our Mind* (Capstone, 2011), 'imagination is the gift of human consciousness. With it we can step away from the here and now, the concrete present'. And yet many people at work use their imagination to visualize disaster and failure rather than a brighter creative future. Learning the skills of relaxation and visualization are of paramount importance to the creative process, as we discovered in Part II.

The challenge for the workplace is how to create the time and space for relaxation so that thinking can take place at all. Google allows its staff an allotted time every week to wander and think. Well, you might say, that's fine for Google but not for us in our pressurized environment. Find a way. That's one of your creative challenges. Take it to the team and use the CREATE problem-solving process outlined in Chapter 14 to come up with a solution.

Play at work

Many of the CEOs I talked to mentioned that they treated business like a game. Now that's not to say that they did not take being employers seriously – they did. But the sport analogy gave me the impression of distancing themselves from the vicissitudes of the business market while at the same time loving what they did.

Ben & Jerry's is a US ice-cream company and a division of the Anglo-Dutch Unilever conglomerate that manufactures ice-cream, frozen yogurt and sorbets. Lifelong friends Ben Cohen and Jerry Greenfield met in seventh grade gym class. In 1977 they completed a correspondence course on ice-cream making from Pennsylvania State University's Creamery. Two things have impressed me: Ben and Jerry's campaigns for what they believe in (same sex marriage, unhappy European cows) always accompanied by a great sense of fun. This is epitomized by their latest campaign to help the plight of the European cow and their limited access to open pasture:

Fresh Water! Better Feed! More Pasture Romps! Cows Are People Too!

Innocent has the same feel.

CASE STUDY

Spotlight on: Innocent

Innocent was founded by three Cambridge University graduates, Richard Reed, Adam Balon and Jon Wright, who were working in consulting and advertising. They were friends at St John's College, Cambridge and in 1999, after spending six months working on smoothie recipes, they sold their drinks at a music festival in London.

Right from the start they had fun with their business. After their inaugural smoothie 'release' people who bought were asked to put their empty bottles in a 'yes' or 'no' bin depending on whether they thought they should quit their jobs to make smoothies. The 'Yes' bin was full, the 'No' bin emptier, so they went back to work the next day and resigned.

I think we quite like, and buy from, the companies that are fun and have fun doing what they do. Might it be different for the more serious professions like law, accountancy or banking? Personally I don't think so. Professional expertise does not decline with enjoyment.

It is so challenging to come up with new ideas that you do have to encourage yourself and others to see things differently. Why not have fun in the process?

Have a look at the 'What if' exercise below. I love it and often ask leadership groups to enact one of their chosen What ifs. The idea is that by going on a flight of fancy you are going beyond your normal hidebound thinking and introducing other possibilities. Minds need as much limbering up as bodies.

What if ...

paper were alive?

e-mails were taxed?

your feet really needed to go to sleep. How long would they need to get a full rest? How would you wake them?

you had just been selected to join the next mission to Mars?

you won the lottery without even buying a ticket?

you could make one of your wishes come true? Which one would you choose?

fish ruled the planet?

▶

◀

> we had never invented guns?
>
> clouds could speak? What would they say?
>
> everyone ate only fruit?
>
> you had 10 fingers on every hand?
>
> fear were replaced with confidence?
>
> pigs did indeed fly?

One of my favourites on the list is the first – 'if paper were alive'. One group asked paper politely if it minded being used and put sheets of paper through a shredder with spine chilling cries of pain. A 'be kind to paper' movement was started. The feedback was that the group became more aware of each page of paper as a precious commodity and an objective was to use less paper in true pursuit of the paperless office.

Some others on the list were just fun. Enjoy and use them in your teams or at meetings to limber people up before brainstorming. Just remember that today's strange ideas can be tomorrow's reality.

Collaborate

Join a group or society that discusses issues of the day or challenges the status quo of your profession. Listening to others is one of the best and most creative ways of thinking differently.

The Creative Problem Solving Institute (CPSI) in the United States, founded by Alex Osborn who invented brainstorming, is where I go each year to be challenged and to replenish my creative juices. There are myriad activities to activate even the most sluggish mind. I have learnt to dance to Brazilian music, sung eight-part harmonies with people who have never sung before, painted a giant group abstract in a squash court to the Brandenburg Concerto and learnt to perform magic tricks from a master. This was achieved not at a single conference of course, but over many years of attendance. All of these experiences free up your creative thinking and get you out of rutted ways of behaving.

I was invited to a team building event in Norway recently. I am just a nursery slope skier but I learnt to toboggan at speed, mainly because I didn't want to let them down by delivering a poor performance. Of course the native Norwegians knew everything there was to know about snow and when we Brits were allocated to teams for the final competition we all wanted to collaborate with the experts.

They knew that if you wanted to leap from tree stump to tree stump without touching the snow, you use planks of wood as bannisters to help you balance. They can light a fire in the snow with no matches. They can leap off mountainsides on things like tea trays and control their descent to the finish line. The marvellous thing was that they helped us gain an expertise that we didn't know we could have. We joined in putting forward ideas that were considered and not rejected. We learnt much ... and had fun. In terms of creativity it enabled me to learn from others and to realize that although this was not my area of expertise I did have a view and my ideas did count.

Include the team

Ideas are like children. Your own are great. Alec Baldwin in 'Charlie Rose'

A friend works for a very successful advertising agency. I commented about the excitement of coming up with new ideas for projects every day. 'Oh,' she said, 'we don't do any of that. The man at the top has the ideas and we deliver them.' So they were hired for their creative nous then turned into lackeys. What a waste! For team creativity, a major limiting factor is a leader's belief that 'my ideas are the only ideas'; a completely ridiculous notion but a prevalent one.

Let's return to Bruce's dilemma with empowerment that we explored at the very start of this chapter, because I think it epitomizes the challenges companies have when trying to introduce creativity to the workplace. 'Ideas generation' is often a task grafted on to away days once a year, or else given to the marketing or strategy department instead of being a way of life. Exploring how to get creative at work, in the workplace, is more beneficial so that creativity becomes like breathing – a rather good habit!

Creative organizations will allow time at every meeting for the discussion of new ideas and problem solving by a team. They will also have some puffy couches and areas where people can gather to discuss issues. Creativity will be featured and talked about at general meetings.

I have worked with many scientific organizations where ideas for new drugs are not only important for company survival in a competitive marketplace but also for us the potential users of such medication. The problem is that these organizations are huge and bureaucratic. As soon as you introduce layers of accountabilities, creativity is stifled. Big challenge. For example, when I started out trying to introduce problem-solving strategies for one scientific organization, I could see that anything too wild or unusual was not going to work. Participants in workshops would close up and become belligerently silent or openly aggressive. 'Why are we doing this exercise?' one scientist asked me. When I replied that it was just for fun to get things going, she looked at me as if I had a number of heads. Too much too soon for her.

Some people did run with the ideas but encountered difficulties when trying to introduce them to their meetings. In a desert of creativity, gradual introduction is important.

How to become more creative every day

Here are some thoughts on how to become creative in your workplace:

- *Mind Map presentations.* It shortens the time for putting ideas together and by placing everything on a page with ideas radiating from a central point you begin to see associations you haven't seen before. Use Mind Mapping when drilling for details on an issue. Use it on a flipchart for all to see. Mind Mapping a business plan places everything on one page of a flipchart and you can store it to be brought out at points throughout the year to ensure you are all on track. It can also be added to and contributions can be welcomed from all.

- *Give yourself time to think.* Cease to be instant in your response to crises. Take five minutes to think through all ramifications. Phone a friend for an alternative view.

- *Brainstorm ideas and problems with your team at each meeting.* Even five minutes at the end will produce creative solutions. Problems do not have to be solved on your own.

What should you stop to allow yourself more time for creativity?

If creativity is so important, something needs to be done to make time for it. When I ask for ideas about freeing up time the major area for discussion is meetings: too many and too boring. Perhaps attendance at these could be reduced or delegated. Starting and finishing meetings on time would help too.

E-mails are another bane of people's lives. Being copied in on everything is so time-consuming as you feel that you must read them all in case you miss something. If you focus on creativity as a priority then you will find a way to make time. We always find time for important things.

How could you and others be rewarded for becoming more creative?

'You get what you reward.' I am not sure who coined the phrase but it is predictive of behaviour. If no one else is going to reward you for new ideas, reward yourself and let a boss or colleague know. Then make sure that your team is rewarded for being creative. Again a small reward – a card, a thank you, a mention at a meeting – is all it takes. These 'people of the month/year' things don't work.

For a whole team to be rewarded, do something 'teamy'. I was working with a group of leadership mentors recently when one said that on a Friday, when his team had hit target or had come up with a solution to a major issue, he would take them to the cinema and have pizza afterwards. There was a stunned silence. Where did he get permission, where did he get the money – had nobody reported him? 'Listen,' he said. 'I produce the goods so no one is going to complain. Anyway the team pay for their cinema ticket and the pizza. The point is we celebrate.' This team leader was promoted to director the following month. You might wait forever to be rewarded by those in charge but you can start rewarding your team or colleagues yourself and see it catch on.

Leadership

I really believe that to foster creativity in any organization the leader has to be a confident person. If not, ideas delivered will be stillborn because a leader lacking in confidence fears failure, won't take risks and might even want to undermine the success of others. To be empowering – truly empowering – risk taking has to be embraced. This chapter brings us full circle to my book, *Confidence at Work* and I would adjure you to read this too (well I would, wouldn't I). It gives readers many interesting tools to benchmark their own leadership behaviour with suggestions on how to fill any gaps.

CASE STUDY

Spotlight on: IBM study

An IBM Global CEO study highlighted creative leadership as a critical capability for success. Sixty per cent of leaders chose creativity as the most important leadership quality over the next five years. A subsequent project examining creative leadership noted that 'creative leaders invite disruptive innovation, encourage others to drop outdated approaches and take balanced risk. They are open minded and inventive in expanding their management and communication styles'.

The researchers also posed the question as to the survival – nay thriving – of some companies during times of change while others are 'blindsided'. They come up with a list of suggestions of what works, and I have selected a few for you to review:

- Companies should evaluate their past culture and appetite for creativity.

- Your organization's breakthrough thinking and projects should be charted for best practice and repeated when necessary.

- Build small diverse teams to pursue bold ideas.

- Institute experiential learning in your leadership team as traditional leadership training does not foster creativity.

- Identify role models who are participative leaders and foster creativity. They are inspirational to the rest of the organization.

I am going to leave you with a couple of examples of good inspirational leadership, from a CEO and a Chairman in charge of different supermarket chains.

In Focus

Asda and 100 ideas

Heather Sharkey used to work with Allan Leighton, the well-known former CEO of Asda. She tells this story of good leadership at work with creativity.

In the late 1990s Asda was researching the way people shopped, mostly females, mothers to be precise. It wanted to try a new layout for displaying its edible and non-edible foods (ie not frozen stuff). They put cameras on shoppers and noticed how they chose their produce. The discovery was that mothers wanted to buy seven sets of meals speedily. So breakfast produce had to be together, crisps, juice, cold meats had to be clustered for lunch and packed lunches and the options of seven evening meals, comprising chicken, mince, cold meats, vegetables and potatoes also had to be displayed together. Fifteen aisles in total had to be changed; a huge undertaking as this was to be replicated up and down the country.

Heather quailed as she was in charge of the roll-out. What if it doesn't work? All that money wasted and customers up in arms when they couldn't find their favourite meals. Allan Leighton asked for her input as to what would work and they came up with a roll-out of just 10 stores to see if it worked as a concept. He told her, 'I'd rather you tried 100 things in the hope of 10 working than trying 10 and one succeeding.' Of course it worked and all stores were changed to the new format.

Heather found his permission to fail inspiring and motivating. As a result, creativity flourished.

In Focus

Superquinn supermarket steps to the workers' side

Superquinn supermarket was founded in 1960 by Feargal Quinn in Dundalk, County Louth, Ireland. Superquinn has always been quirky with a focus on customer feedback and wacky competitions. For example, it had a running challenge to highlight the most unusual places customers would take Superquinn carrier bags. The bags had to be photographed – attached to people of course and not blowing in the wind. These bags reached the Great Wall of China, the Himalayas and various other wonders of the world. All photographs were featured on the walls of the supermarket.

One day, the checkout staff revolted. Their representatives argued that their members needed better chairs if they were to sit there for hours at a time. Management argued that the chairs were fine and confrontation loomed. The CFO was worried. Disruptive strike action would cost a fortune and while the organization could no doubt 'win' the dispute, it could well prove to be a pyrrhic victory.

The chairman of the group was well known to the workforce. Unconventionally, he often donned a white coat and served at the butcher's counter. He had even been known to stack a shelf or two. He was on first-name terms with staff in many of the branches. He bitterly regretted that his young management team had let matters deteriorate to the point where they might have their first industrial action in the company's 50 year history.

However, he also knew that it would be imprudent to impose a solution on his management team. As he walked the floor chatting to customers and staff he had a brainwave. At the next board meeting he did something he hardly ever did. He made a pronouncement. All board members, including himself, were to spend one whole day in the course of the following month on the checkout. He felt it would give them 'grass roots' insight into how and what people were buying as well as being informative. Everyone readily agreed.

▶

◀

> At the following month's meeting the CFO – who had previously vociferously opposed new chairs for staff – put forward a compelling case for new seats on medical grounds, citing the possible days off with bad backs as more than justification for the purchase. The chairman was delighted.

Steps to creativity at work

✩ Make sure you have the energy, curiosity and courage to be creative.

✩ Ask those around you about your ability to empower. Are you a micro-manager or do you coach others to a better performance by finding answers themselves?

✩ If a leader, do you ask your team for input to problems, challenges and business plans? Think back to Swan Vestas and blind manufacturing: it was staff at the sharp end, doing the work, who can have the small ideas that make a huge difference. Never forget who does the work and visit them often.

✩ Be prepared to take the risks attached to new ideas.

✩ Have the humility to realize that you don't have all the answers.

Using a creative process

The story so far ...

We now know that we are all built for creativity with an ability to have 'aha' moments. We are all creative in different ways: foraging, exploring, synthesizing or disseminating. We know that there are certain circumstances that are conducive to creativity, like the adjacent possible and the ideal Q. We know that creativity at work is about combining, changing, or reapplying existing ideas. We know that simple, small, practical ideas that no one seems to have thought of yet can save or create fortunes. We know there are skills that help to foster creativity in ourselves and others like empowerment, courage, curiosity and good leadership.

But we also know that companies – British or US, European or Asian – are not systematically grasping the creativity nettle so that it is embedded in the company culture. So in Part V we are going to look at a few processes that can produce creative results when you need them. You will be introduced to the CREATE process for ideas and twisting, noodling, and hatching as techniques to get the best out of ideas.

Creative thinking can be scary

Creative thinking does not rely on past experience or known facts. It is about visualizing a new product or a new future for ourselves and others and working out how to get there. It is about exploring possibilities, the 'what if' of the imagination. It is amorphous, ambiguous, open ended ... and a bit scary if you have never encountered or never been given the permission to pursue that kind of thinking.

It is certainly not typical thinking found in the workplace where there are finite outcomes, focused aims and objectives with performance indicators and monitoring. So I can understand why there is a reluctance to embrace creative thinking with its whiff of the insurgent about it. Once unleashed, how can you control it? This is a legitimate question as you can't just let the creatives take over the workplace so that *every* idea is pursued in the hope that one works. Some judgement is necessary.

On reflection I believe that the scariness of creative thinking leads to two reactions from organizations. 1) They hand over the mantle to research and development departments which are tasked with coming up with new ways of doing things. Or since everything is now online, the IT department is landed with 'leading edge' initiatives. 2) They invite creative consultants to facilitate the new business plan, future company strategy, change programme or new product development – and then disappear.

This 'peripheral' input insulates creativity from the rest of the organization. It might be very helpful, but leaving creativity to others misses a trick. Those who are part of the company, who are carrying out the work, probably have 25 ideas a day but no one has asked them for their input and so their creativity never sees the light of day. And since we know that everyone is creative, just in different ways, why wouldn't you tap into this resource on your doorstep?

A colleague was telling me that her company had hired an impressive group of American consultants at great expense to help each department with their business planning. Her group was very receptive to what the consultants were trying to achieve and produced some interesting ideas for the next financial year. When I asked if her group were using any of the techniques initiated by the consultants or whether they had integrated creativity into their meetings on a regular basis, she told me reluctantly that they had not. They hadn't been trained or encouraged to do that. What a lot of money to spend on a missed opportunity.

A bit like the telecoms company we explored in Chapter 12, which empowered an untrained shop floor so that they spent all their time in meetings, not producing phones, any organization that embraces creativity without developing the three ingredients shown in Figure 13.1 is doomed to failure.

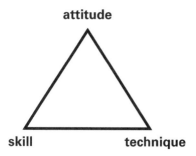

Figure 13.1 The three ingredients for integrating creativity

Three ingredients for integrating creativity into organizations

1. Attitude

- An attitude of inclusion and diversity.
- Provision of critical feedback in a positive framework.

- Rewarding failure to encourage ideas.
- Tolerance of risk to pilot the new.

2. Technique

- Mind Mapping to enable issue finding.
- 'What if' techniques to future plan.
- Framing questions – how might we ...?
- Brainstorming.

3. Skill

- Assessing teams for creative styles.
- Assessing ideas for utility.
- Dissemination of solutions and actions.
- Using a creative process.

Any organization requires all three to succeed creatively but the skill of using a creative process is for me of paramount importance. I get the feeling that companies would like people to come up with innovative ideas without recourse to creativity; this relates to 'Data to decision making' that I mentioned in Part I.

IBM published its research about cultivating organizational creativity in 2011. I heard the presentation by two of the researchers and unfortunately they looked like two be-suited accountants, which was curiously at odds with their message of creative exploration. The message was about letting the creative potential of employees flourish by means of collaboration, social networks and sharing of information. But when pressed about the use of a creative process the reply was swift: 'We see no need for that.'

Creative process

Any creative process that generates ideas and helps to solve problems focuses on two different types of thinking: exploratory and critical. The latter is more prevalent in the workplace than the non-judgmental freer kind of thinking associated with creativity.

In an activity like problem solving, both kinds of thinking are important. It's not a case of either or. First, you must analyse the problem, then generate possible solutions, next choosing and implementing the best solution and finally evaluating the effectiveness of the solution. This process alternates between the two kinds of thinking, the exploratory and the critical:

Critical thinking	Exploratory thinking
analytic	generative
convergent	divergent
vertical	lateral
probability	possibility
judgement focused	judgement suspended
objective	subjective
linear	associative
reasoning	novelty
yes but ...	yes and ...

To practise using both types of thinking a favourite exercise of mine helps address work issues on a continuous basis. It is called the Bug List and is very simple.

The Bug List

At meetings, perhaps at the end, ask the group to think about any issues that might have occurred that week:

- What are all the things that bug or concern you about your work?
- Choose three or four that you could work on.
- Take five minutes to consider how might you zap these and come up with an attack plan.

This simple system can be used on a weekly basis or on a Monday and then revisited on a Friday. There are a couple of good outcomes: the group is in charge of their own bug zappers and target any problems arising quickly, before they become entrenched. It strikes at the heart of happiness at work, helping to generate an atmosphere conducive to creativity at work. The group may come up with a number of zappers so you can introduce the democratic process of a show of hands for the zap of choice. It also allows the group to practise exploratory thinking when they list all issues, using something like Table 13.1, and critical thinking when they choose what to work on.

Table 13.1 The bug list attack plan

Bugs	Zap attack!
1	1
2	2
3	3
4	4
5	5

Steps to creativity at work

☆ Bring your creative thinking in house.

☆ Ensure you have the three ingredients for integrating creativity into your organization: attitude, technique and skill.

☆ Be aware of exploratory and critical thinking as a basis for creativity at work.

☆ Use the bug list for quick fix solutions.

The CREATE process

Generating ideas and solving problems

Once your colleagues are comfortable with confronting and overcoming everyday issues at meetings, you can introduce an ideas generation and problem solving process.

It is surprising how few business meetings contain creative problem solving. Sitting passively listening to a series of presentations, the chairman pontificating and the finance director number crunching, with actions no one agrees to and certainly intends to do nothing about, still seems to be the norm. Of course spread sheets are important and presentations are useful but they are not sufficient to involve and motivate those attending. The problem-solving process called CREATE, shown in Figure 14.1, could signify the end to these boring meetings.

Before going into the details of this process, an overview of what is entailed might be useful. The whole idea with problem solving is that, in sequence, you open up discussions using divergent techniques like brainstorming and Mind Mapping, then home in on priorities or actions. The whole thing looks like a series of fish tails. At each stage of CREATE, divergent tools are used first, followed by the convergent; in other words opening

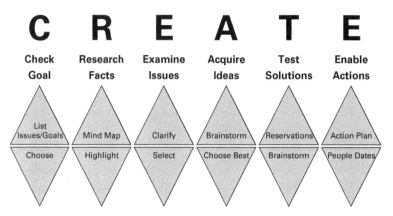

Figure 14.1 CREATE – the problem-solving process

up ideas then closing in on the ones that suit, fit the context or are do-able.

1. Check goals

Figure 14.2

The whole process starts by opening up discussion about what you want to achieve or any issues the team has. Do this by simply asking them what goal or challenge is facing them and putting the replies on a flipchart. But of course even in the best of groups some people contribute more than others. A technique that helps is to ask people to write their suggestions on Post-It notes which are then stuck on the flipchart or wall. Someone then clusters them into similar topics. This is a particularly useful for a group who are shy.

I will talk about three recent CREATE sessions I ran with groups of headteachers, lawyers and scientists to show how the process might work. This first step clarifies the area for the group to work on, and achieves buy-in as all ideas are listed. Some prompt questions might be:

- What goals do you want to accomplish this year?

- What challenges do you face?

- What do you wish worked better?

Once you have written a list of all possible areas for discussion on a flipchart or whiteboard, ask the group to select the goal or issue that is most important to them, that they can influence directly or requires a new look. You can achieve convergence by giving everyone two ticks, which they can place beside the list of topics, or a simple show of hands can work.

A recent CREATE session I undertook with headteachers had two pages of a flipchart full of goals. These topics were wide ranging, including school leadership, safe parking, negative teaching assistants, improving grotty parts of schools and pupil progress.

The *headteachers* chose to work on pupil progress.

A *large law firm* wanted to look at profitability and, out of a list of topics, chose acquiring more customers.

A *group of scientists* in a pharmaceutical company wanted to reduce their stress at work. From a multitude of topics, they chose relaxation as the one they wanted to progress.

Everyone now is clear about what needs to be tackled and can move to section two of the process. Without going through this initial process, the group could have ended up dealing with too broad an issue or goal, or one imposed by the group leaders. I cannot count the number of times I have had to stop a leader making up the group's minds for them during this process – usually during a course on empowerment!

2. Research facts

The next step involves researching everything about the goal or issue. Remember you
are not focusing on solutions but still con-
centrating on the problem. There is a strong
tendency to want to solve instantly rather
than explore. Curb that enthusiasm at this
stage. Read the story below for a good
example of how, without research, you can
be trying to solve the wrong problem.

Figure 14.3

In Focus

United Distillers (now Diageo)

The major drinks producer United Distillers, now Diageo, had a
problem. One of its premier brands was not performing as expected
in New York City. It cared about this because NYC was a heartland
for its core demographic. If it wasn't doing well in the Big Apple it
might well bomb everywhere else.

The company was puzzled. Nothing had changed about the drink.
In fact – and worse still – the consumer panel reports it had
immediately commissioned all showed high degrees of satisfaction
with the product. So a product everybody liked was flopping in the
bar. What was wrong?

The knee-jerk response was to throw money at the problem. 'Let's
advertise' was the mantra round the darkened table of the smoke-
filled room. The VP of Marketing stood firm. 'Why advertise? We have
the best brand recognition in the business. People know about us.
It's what we don't know about the people that's the problem.'

The conventional wisdom now was that a large firm of consultants
should be brought in, reports written, strategies unfolded. Time,
and above all money, spent. The Marketing VP resisted these
blandishments. Then somebody said, 'Why don't we all go for a drink?'

▶

◀

'Our main product is tanking and you want to go to a bar?'

'Last time I looked, that's where we sold it ....'

In fact, they split up and went to several bars. They didn't drink much but sat and watched and listened. Back in the office, they pooled notes. At first, there was no clear picture – everything seemed normal. But slowly, as they worked through their process time and time again, a common factor emerged.

In New York people don't usually order Scotch by brand – they ask for 'a Scotch'. 'So which Scotch do they get?' asked VP of Marketing. Someone named a competitor's brand. 'No,' he replied decisively. 'They get the one nearest to him!' Then it all became clear. The company was marketing well. It was delivering to the premises and selling at competitive wholesale prices but unless a customer specified its brand by name, he or she got a Scotch – the one closest to the bartender.

So what did the company do? It went into the bars and aggressively marketed a lit bar display showcasing its products. It gave it away. It also made it just big enough to ensure that it would only fit in the middle of most bars and so was more prominent. Then in a stroke of creative genius, the company went one step further. It created what it called 'The Bartenders' Guild' based of course around its products, and so built loyalty. The bartenders got a free product familiarization course and upon completion they all got a pin to show what a distinguished bar person they were.

So now, when someone in one of the target premises in New York said he or she would like 'a Scotch', chances were that the (now) loyal bartender would say, 'Have you tried X? It's very good.' Cheers to good research paying off in the end!

I find mind mapping is a good technique at this stage for interrogating and displaying all underlying issues and areas of further exploration. A group can view the whole set of circumstances and then choose which strand or strands require more delving and understanding. Issues are explored to expand knowledge and understanding of the goal. The team then chooses the section that they want to delve into even further.

The *headteachers* who chose pupil progress as a goal decided that they could achieve the biggest difference by focusing on disadvantaged children.

When the *scientists* who wanted to reduce their stress at work discussed their stress issues and a desire for relaxation, they discovered it was the constant presentations to senior management that caused them the most problems.

For the *group of lawyers,* the goal selected was acquiring new customers. When the issues were explored by Mind Mapping, the administrators present complained that they had no time to deal with new clients. Time was the issue that had to be explored further.

3. Examine issues

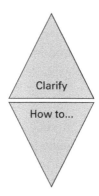

Figure 14.4

Look at the group's selected problem or goal and view it from all angles, for example how to make it better, how it might look, in what ways it might be changed, the additional aspects that could be considered.

A *twisting* technique helps here. Turn things on their head. If you did nothing, what would happen to the problem? If you weren't a teacher, lawyer, scientist, how might you view the problem? If you were a Martian what might you think? Think about your goal or issue differently or from every angle. Twist it upside down and end up with a 'how to' statement.

The *headteachers* asked how they could help the most vulnerable children.

For the *scientists* their statement was: 'How to delegate presentations.'

And the *lawyers'* was: 'How to create more time to accommodate new clients.'

This section makes sure that the problem selected is really the one that will make a difference.

4. Acquire ideas

Figure 14.5

Stage 4 is where the group brainstorms as many ideas as they can in two minutes. Wild ideas are best as they move you far away from what has been done before.

Getting people into the right frame of mind for brainstorming can take some time. The majority of our day if not our lives is taken up with logical thinking and giving reasons for our actions. We need to leave all of that behind as creativity thrives on spontaneity and relaxation, so it's a good idea to start with a mental limbering up exercise.

Mental limbering up

You could brainstorm anything; how many uses can you, as a group, come up with in two minutes for one of the following:

- a truck of damaged ping pong balls;
- old used light bulbs;
- 1,000 toilet rolls;
- a brick.

Frankly, you could choose anything. It is better if it isn't anything work related so that there is no professional expertise necessary for the outcome; this helps free responses. To increase the fun, reward the team with prizes for the most ideas, reinforcing quantity over quality.

After mental limbering up return to the 'how to' question in hand and remind participants of the guidelines of brainstorming as there can be a tendency to return to critical thinking when a real issue appears.

Guidelines for brainstorming

- Go for quantity not quality.

- Don't worry about making mistakes or coming up with the right answer; just go for as many ideas as possible. The time for analysis is later.

- Do not be judgemental.

- There are no right or wrong answers.

- Freewheel with thoughts and ideas. Just keep the momentum going with the first thing that comes into your head.

- The faster the pace the better.

- Make connections.

- Piggyback on others' ideas. Use them as prompts.

Once all ideas are charted, within two minutes the group chooses the best idea. Was it a very practical choice? Or was it a more outrageous idea? The latter is probably the better to pursue. In other words it is the unusual, weird, off-the-wall idea that you can modify to become something do-able. The ordinary or commonplace has probably been done before and therefore will never be ground-breaking.

The *headteachers* came up with 'pester power against parents.'

The *lawyers* – 'set fire to all old equipment'.

The *scientists* – 'go on presentation strike'.

5. Test solutions

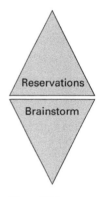

Figure 14.6

If the guidelines for the brainstorming of Stage 4 suggest being non-judgemental and exploratory, then Stage 5 is about critical, analytical thinking. None of the ideas from our three groups above is particularly do-able so:

How might these ideas be improved? How might a wild idea be tamed?

What could they really see themselves doing?

What reservations might they have about implementation?

A *noodling* technique helps here. When faced with wild solutions, don't cast them away. Talk about your reservations and then ask what might be good about the solution because there may be something useful even in the most extreme ideas.

Example problem: How can we get college students to learn grammar?

Solution: Spank their bottoms. This is pretty wild, partly because it's probably illegal. But should we just throw it out? Why not ask what's good about it?

Noodling answers:

- It gives individual attention to the poor performers.

- It is a form of motivation.

- It is easy and costs nothing.

The next question is: can we adapt or incorporate some of these good things into an interesting, more do-able solution? After noodling to a more do-able solution, brainstorm ways in which this idea could be incorporated into working practice.

The *headteachers'* idea for 'pester power' for parents noodled into rewarding the parents for their involvement in the school – coffee mornings, crèche facilities, language classes or other skills sessions – all sponsored and free.

The *lawyers* went from 'setting fire to all equipment' to noodling that their computers and photocopiers and all back office equipment required updating, all of which needed to be done before a sales drive for more clients.

The *scientists* went from 'going on presentation strike' into getting younger members of staff to present in front of the board of directors. This way they would realize that other team members could deliver the data, not just the heads of departments.

6. Enable actions

This is the final step of the process but one that can take the longest time as it involves the institution of an action plan and the dissemination of a solution:

Figure 14.7

- What are all the action steps that can be taken to implement the solution?

- Who will undertake to do what and by when?

- What responsibilities need to be allocated, funds distributed?

- Install a mechanism to evaluate success or failure.

- Establish a timeline and a set of objectives when the idea or solution is proved to work or when it should be terminated.

Making sure action plans are acted upon is a major role for someone in a team. The Synthesizers and Disseminators come into their own, especially at this stage of the creativity game. Of course you need to get the whole team to complete the creative style questionnaire to identify these people (see Table 4.1 on page 31).

Synthesizers and Disseminators should be put in charge of collecting, filing and instituting ideas. None should be lost and where ideas or solutions are implemented it is very important that the individual or teams who generated them are remembered and recognized. 'Why bother' is often the cry from staff whose ideas have either been ignored or put in place and saved fortunes with no thanks or acknowledgement.

It is at this stage that good presentation skills are paramount to obtain buy-in, and a degree of risk taking has to be tolerated for the piloting of ideas. Of course there are no guarantees that, despite going through the CREATE process, robust though it is, every new idea or solution will work. It could be the wrong time for an idea to take root, it could be too expensive to roll out, or it could work in one environment but not in another. An example of an idea that worked in Italy but not in the United States despite enthusiastic implementation is outlined below. The trick with a potential dud ... fast failure!

In Focus

Howard Schultz and fast failure

Howard Schultz, to boost the ailing fortunes of Starbucks, came up with idea of selling yoghurt ice cream in his stores. It was a product he had experienced on a visit to Italy. He loved it and bought the very expensive equipment on his return to the United

▶

States. The equipment was installed in all stores in the U.S. and staff were trained how to use it and clean it. Cleaning it was very important because, if not pristine, this machine would start to smell. Staff had to make sure it was odour-free in the mornings and at night. It was adding hours on to already long days and even with their best efforts at cleanliness there still lurked a milky odour that was starting to overwhelm the coffee aroma. Even worse, the public didn't buy it.

Three months after buying and installing the yoghurt machines Howard Schultz ordered their removal. 'Well,' he said, 'it was fast failure. You win some you lose some.'

He kept a close watch over the sales as well as the other downsides of cleaning and odour and when it ceased to stack up he pulled it immediately. He mentioned that some organizations hang on to practices that have ceased to be useful a very long time ago in a kind of 'wishful' thinking. He lost a few million on that deal but his instant coffee, which has taken 20 years to perfect, will net him a billion dollars next year.

The moral of this story is to try new ideas, closely monitor the outcomes and pull swiftly if not hitting target. Rollout if successful. Then try the next ... and the next.

Outcomes of CREATE

It is worth charting the journey of the original idea to the end product. It is always a surprise:

'Pupil progress' started the *headteachers'* CREATE process and they ended up wanting to incentivize parents of more vulnerable pupils to involve themselves in the school. This is underway.

The goal of 'more clients' for the *lawyers* ended up with an entire update of their back office equipment to speed up current client delivery. This took place and now they are ready for a new business drive.

The 'relaxation' objective of the *scientists* progressed to getting younger members of staff to present to the Board of Directors so they, as much as the senior scientists, would be asked to carry out presentations. This initiative continued until the pharmaceutical company was taken over last year.

Hatching

These ideas and solutions may require further thought and work. A process I call hatching, like an egg, requires the idea to be placed in the back of the mind, slept upon and then re-examined. The time to hatch is when there is the germ of something good but it is perhaps not compelling enough, not different enough. The *idea traction list* is a good rule of thumb, and if the chosen solution doesn't quite hit that spot then go into hatching mode. Leave it alone and revisit with fresh eyes around the meeting room table perhaps.

Idea traction

It should be simple.

It should surprise.

It should be concrete and able to be described.

It should be credible.

It should make a difference.

Where an organization rewards the generation of ideas and has a process to capture them then, like buses, there will be others along in a moment.

Advantages of the CREATE process

Everyone is involved in the process and what you end up brainstorming and seeking solutions for is often a surprise but is usually the best fit for the problem. You achieve greater buy-in when everyone considers reservations and noodles the solution together. Everyone gets the chance to be creative, and the more you practise the process the more quickly you get ideas.

Steps to creativity at work

☆ Start a creative process by using the Bug List with teams and at every meeting. It teaches exploratory and critical thinking.

☆ Use the CREATE process at every opportunity at work. You will have fresh ideas every time.

☆ Ensure that you and the team have the attitude, technique and skill to be creative at work.

The final fling

I t's the final fling, the feet up at the end of the journey and time to reflect.

I set out some common preconceptions when I introduced this book – some myths about creativity at work:

- *Creative people, even those at work, are eccentrics and different from the rest of us.* I certainly discovered, with the artists and opera directors I interviewed, that they had a distinctive curiosity and way of adapting what they perceived in the world. But they weren't weird. And creative people at work that I met and interviewed focused their creativity on adaptation of products and processes for the good of their organizations. Nothing *outré* there.

- *Creativity is really about the arts and has no place in everyday life* and certainly not in either business or the professions. The results of my 100 interviews tended to reinforce this preconception. It is alive and well. But at the same time as my interviewees were adhering to this myth they were telling me about creative ideas that they had about their work. So clearly ideas do not constitute creativity in their eyes. But of course they do. The brain's 'ahas' light up as evidence.

- *Creativity is a mysterious process that can't be studied* as ideas come out of the blue with no traceable path. This is palpably untrue: with MRI scans and electro-encephalograms creativity can now be charted. We also know that creativity is not just the preserve of the right brain. Left brain activity related to language and stories is equally creative.

- *The greatest creativity comes from people working on their own,* witness Archimedes and Sir Isaac Newton. We know this to be untrue, from research into ideal Q in the theatre world and its implications for diversity in teams. And what about the reinstated glory of brainstorming in teams? What can be more exciting than sharing and building on ideas in a team of different creative styles and achieving solutions as a result of that collaboration. What might look like the lone breakthrough could in most cases be traced back to a plethora of influences from others.

- *It might be ok for the Googles of this world* that have money to throw at creativity but not me in my small business. Attitude, technique and skill are far better resources than money for creative endeavours. Much can be learnt from Google but all can be adapted for our use whatever the size of our enterprise.

So the myths have been busted, but just as I was about to finish my reflections I noticed in my inbox that psychologist Adrian Furnham, Professor of Psychology at the University of London, had spoken at an innovation conference in Greece. He claimed that you can't teach people to be creative and you really don't want creative people anywhere near your business. I of course couldn't disagree more. So reluctantly I must add another myth to the list:

- *You can't teach people to be creative.*

When I was working with leaders in a pharmaceutical company in the United States they were wary of anything to do with creativity and problem solving. The nature of many of their scientific jobs is to be compliant in the following of procedure, as FDA approval is the goal against which everything is set. But that doesn't mean they can't have ideas about how they present information, how they run their teams and how they utilize resources. After initial sessions that involved investigating issues and brainstorming ways around them, these scientists kept asking for more input on creativity and ways they could integrate it with their teams. Many advanced creativity courses and alumni events ensued as this group began to see the utility of these skills.

As for working with 'creatives' in business, ie the Explorers in style terms, these people will be less organized than their colleagues, more inclined to conceptual thinking than action. That comes with the territory. However, assist them with a Synthesizer or Disseminator and their output will be translated into do-able projects. A blueprint for that can be seen in the Google Spotlight (in Chapter 9) where executive chairman Eric Schmidt took away any organizational and commercial pressure from Sergei Brin and Larry Page to allow them to do what they do so well. We can't be all things to all people, so it is important that we know the creative styles around us at work and manage them accordingly.

So with these myths busted let me reflect on what have been the highlights of my journey through the landscape of creativity. The first for me is just how emotional and knee jerk so much of our thinking and decision making is. To be truly rational and in control of decisions that will shape our work lives, we need to understand the many thinking pitfalls to which we can succumb. The only way to get to grips with this is to analyse past decisions that went well and others that were complete fiascos. Organizations (and people) paper over the cracks of these bad decisions with tales of bad markets or poor employee performance. Charting these decisions unemotionally can unleash much corporate learning. Now add the ability to use a process like CREATE to ensure team involvement and objectivity and the results will be breathtakingly different.

The next is that 70 to 80 per cent of my creativity survey takers revealed that their organizations did not have creativity at the top of their agendas and that creativity is not being pursued consistently. And what about the agriculture sector topping the poll on all measures of creativity? It seems that doing things differently is more alive and well down on the farm than anywhere else as they are problem solving continuously.

My favourite creativity concepts are the adjacent possible and the ideal Q. Both guide my own creative thinking and also my development of others. Teresa Amabile, with her power of small wins and how positive feedback can last as long as two days with the outcome of increased creativity at work, has huge implications for modern leadership.

In conclusion I would love you to try some of these ideas; processes like CREATE, games like 'what if' and questionnaires revealing creative styles and creativity surveys. This book is at heart a practical guide, so use it.

Take creativity seriously at work and have fun doing it!

Index